I0824888

Lessons from Bobby

Ten Reasons Robert F. Kennedy Still Matters

Chris Matthews

SIMON & SCHUSTER
New York Amsterdam/Antwerp London
Toronto Sydney/Melbourne New Delhi

Simon & Schuster
1230 Avenue of the Americas
New York, NY 10020

First Simon & Schuster hardcover edition November 2025

Interior design by Silverglass

Manufactured in the United States of America

1 3 5 7 9 10 8 6 4 2

Library of Congress Control Number: 2025945441

ISBN 978-1-6680-1093-8
ISBN 978-1-6680-1095-2 (ebook)

If there was one politician, one person who I thought could hold the community together and continue to give Black people and poor people in the country a sense of hope, that is Robert Kennedy.

—John Lewis, 1968

Contents

Introduction 1

1. Heal the Divide 3

2. Have Some Guts 13

3. Admit Your Mistakes 21

4. Pursue Ideals 29

5. Uphold Human Rights 37

6. Seek Peace 47

7. Enforce the Law 55

8. Be Tough 63

9. Know When to Concede 73

10. Sacrifice 83

Note on Sources 93

Appendix: The Speeches 95

Acknowledgments 161

Lessons from Bobby

Introduction

Robert Francis Kennedy, shot and killed at age forty-two in 1968, was born on November 20, 1925. One hundred years later, his moral leadership matters more than ever.

I was witness to Bobby Kennedy's rise to national prominence, to the strong feelings so many Americans had for him. I am witness today to how faithfully many of those people remember him.

The brilliant 1960 campaign he ran for his brother President Kennedy is deep in my memory. So is the fight for civil rights that Jack and Bobby Kennedy waged alongside Martin Luther King Jr. for this country. The deaths of these great men are etched in our shared American history.

Bobby Kennedy was thirty-five when his brother named him US attorney general. I was fifteen, watching all this from the sidelines. Decades later I relived those Kennedy years in three major books I authored on Jack and Bobby.

The assassination of John F. Kennedy, which took place when I was a college student at Holy Cross, changed my life. The same political violence five years later cost us the lives of Martin Luther King Jr. and Robert F. Kennedy.

Bobby Kennedy was a man of strong personal character. He pursued his ideals, took risks for peace. His greatest legacy was his unique ability to unite Black and white working people in ways not seen since.

Look at our country today, at our wide and deepening divisions. It's time for all of us to revisit Bobby Kennedy and his moral vision. On his 2025 centennial, here are ten of his timeless lessons. Take this book as your personal road map. Its message is clear: America is great when it tries, at its best, to be *good*.

1

Heal the Divide

America is divided. When was the last time you heard that marvelous phrase *e pluribus unum*? "Out of many, one." I know it's on our currency, but how about hearing it from our leaders? When was the last time you heard a politician from either party speak honestly about bringing the country together? About uniting the forces that throw us against one another?

Even families are at war. Thanksgiving dinners are now minefields. Brothers and brothers-in-law can be quick to the trigger. The slightest, most glancing comments for or against President Trump or his MAGA supporters can instantly incite outrage.

One side, obediently loyal to Donald Trump, agrees to everything their leader imagines. The US Senate, once called "the world's greatest deliberative body," bows daily in submission. President Trump names cabinet members—or federal judges—and the Senate genuflects.

Meanwhile, the opposition Democrats are weak, implausibly so. Their favorability ratings stand at the lowest on public record. The party leadership appears to be in chaos, with only an outward fringe offering any true resistance.

What happened to our great Constitution? That exquisite tension we celebrated among the three branches of government—the executive, the legislative, and the court system? Instead, one man calls the shots. In this twenty-first century, the United States of America mimics the same monarchy we revolted against 250 years ago.

One of the factors that weakens us is a variant of what we once called "town vs. gown." It puts working people into one class, the college kids in another. That's become an electoral divide as well. It's what threatens civil unrest, as I said, even at the family dinner table.

This is why Bobby Kennedy matters.

....

I remember watching the funeral train that grim Saturday, June 8, 1968. It was carrying RFK's body from New York's St. Patrick's Cathedral to join his brother in Arlington National Cemetery.

I looked at the faces of those along the tracks, white and Black. Did you ever notice that people who live closest to the rail tracks are, regardless of their skin color, still among our country's poorest? And on that humid day in 1968, both white and Black people stood at attention as this good man made his final way past. I treasure those pictures because they are America at its most needy but also at its best. I can recall the crowd of African Americans in Philadelphia singing "Battle Hymn of the Republic" and the solemn salutes of the white working class gathered between the cities. Their patriotism and hope in a leader could not have stood higher than it did that grim day.

Take a look back at those stark photos today, of white and Black mourners honoring the one leader they hoped could unite them as Americans. At the forlorn faces of the white crowds, the depressed looks on the faces of African Americans. At the one man who had given them the promise of a "better life."

Robert F. Kennedy was killed trying to end the war in Vietnam. He wanted to redirect American priorities from a conflict in Southeast Asia to the problems back here at home. That change of *policy* was why he challenged President Lyndon Johnson that March in the first place.

But there is something else at work in those pictures from the late sixties. He was trying desperately to *unite* us.

Let's agree. The division in our country has gotten way too personal. As I mentioned, one line of separation is between working people and the college crowd. Race is another powerful divider. But back in 1968, the pictures of Black and white faces along the funeral tracks show their common hopes for one man, Bobby Kennedy.

....

Despite his reputation as a "ruthless" partisan defender of his brother Jack, an ally of the Communist-hunting Senator Joseph McCarthy, and a hard-nosed fighter of mobsters on the Senate Rackets Committee, there were early signs of Bobby's promise.

Ken O'Donnell, who captained their Harvard football team, recalled him as the Kennedy brother with the biggest heart. Historian Arthur M. Schlesinger Jr., who knew both Jack and Bobby Kennedy, saw him as a political *romantic*.

There is powerful evidence to back up these claims.

"I was the seventh of nine children," Bobby himself said, "and when you come from that far down you have to struggle to survive." He was also the "runt of the litter," as his father called him, standing far shorter than his handsomer brothers Joe Jr., Jack, and even Ted, all six feet or taller.

Bobby had reason to complain about the unfairness of life. At Milton Academy, he was the rare Roman Catholic. When he joined the US Navy it was as an enlisted man, a common seaman. This was compared to his older brothers Joe Jr. and Jack, who were commissioned officers. At Harvard, he rejected the elite social clubs. He preferred to hang with the jocks at the Varsity Club. It was there in Cambridge that Bobby learned that a Catholic priest, the reverend Leonard Feeney, was preaching the doctrine of "no salvation outside the church." Bobby told his father, Joseph Kennedy, about what he had heard Feeney preaching. His father then reported what his son had just told him to Cardinal Richard Cushing. Having confirmed Bobby's account, Cushing had Feeney removed from the pulpit. Father Feeney was later excommunicated. I can remember the sister at our class at St. Christopher School in Philadelphia instructing us to cross out Feeney's verses from our assigned book of poetry.

I became aware of Bobby's sympathies most personally when I served briefly with the US Capitol Police. It was a patronage appointment I received just after my return from two years with the Peace Corps. It was how I learned that Senator Robert F. Kennedy of New York set himself apart from other senators. Bobby made it a point to greet each of the Capitol Police when he came to work in the morning. Frank Mankiewicz, his Senate press secretary, confirmed that small but important point to me. "He loved cops." No one could call this guy from one of the country's most prominent families an elitist. As someone who began his political career working for the Capitol Police, I loved this story.

This was five decades before that same Capitol Police force sacrificed lives on January 6, 2021, to save members of Congress—and a vice president—from the snarling, violent mob, attackers led by President Trump, who later pardoned every one of them.

As I said, mine was a patronage appointment to the Capitol Police. I had a US senator as my sponsor, who later made me a legislative assistant. Most of the other officers were working guys. Retired from the service, many had been in the army and marines. Many had been MPs, military policemen.

One was Leroy Taylor. He took it upon himself to explain to me the class division in our society, which has recently merged with our politics. I am talking about the new political divide between the college crowd and the much larger class of working people.

One day, that country boy from West Virginia, Leroy Taylor, who had spent years as a hard-nosed MP, decided to fill me in on the difference between me, an obvious college guy, and the working men who made up most of the Capitol Police.

"Do you know why the little man loves his country, Chris?" he asked after calling me aside.

Not knowing what to expect, I said I didn't.

"Because it's all he's *got*."

I have never forgotten those words of Leroy Taylor. I hope I never will.

They define the people who don't have fine houses, or kids heading off to college. What they have is their country; they are determined to protect it.

This is why Bobby Kennedy, born on November 20, 1925, shot by an assassin on June 5, 1968, dead the next day, matters.

....

Today we need an American leader, in fact lots of them, who tries to bring us together. When Bobby Kennedy campaigned in the 1968 presidential primaries, he made a point of doing just that. Contending in the Indiana presidential primary, he campaigned in the city of Gary riding in an open convertible. He sat between Richard Hatcher, Gary's first African American mayor, and middleweight boxing champion Tony Zale, the city's most famous citizen. Bobby intended that as a statement of racial unity.

He ended the day with his own hands bloody, cuff links and shoes missing, so frenzied were the fans who reached for him. "I don't like it," he said of such close-contact campaigning, yet he saw its advantage: "But people can have heard everything about a candidate; and it's the touching him they never forget."

Times are much angrier today. The days when moderate voters could find something good in both the Democratic and Republican parties are gone. That's largely vanished. Out of fifty states, just three—Maine, Pennsylvania, and Wisconsin—have split-party Senate delegations—one Democratic senator and one Republican. The "split ticket" I grew up with lives mainly in people's memories.

How can we get anything done with this kind of division, between those with the good fortune to earn a college degree and those who didn't? And between Black and white people? Not without leaders who can bridge the political and social gap that separates the country itself.

2

Have Some Guts

The most common sight in Washington, DC, is that of US senators afraid to do their job. As John F. Kennedy wrote in *Profiles in Courage*, “The virus of Potomac Fever, which rages everywhere in Washington, breeds nowhere in more virulent form than on the Senate floor. The prospect of forced retirement from ‘the most exclusive club in the world,’ the possibilities of giving up the interesting work, the fascinating trappings and the impressive prerogatives of Congressional office, can cause even the most courageous politician serious loss of sleep.”

Today there are US senators voting in obedience to President Trump after hearing little more than a peep from the White House. Donald Trump can whisper about putting up a candidate to primary an elected senator. Then you don’t hear another word from the august public servant.

Vote for Pete Hegseth as defense secretary? No problem. Approve Trump's whole motley crew of cabinet appointments? "Count me in!" yells each and every GOP lawmaker.

Just a year ago, the US Senate prized its constitutional duty to offer "advice and consent" on a presidential appointment. In 2025, a Trump appointee to the executive—or even the judicial—branch automatically gets the job.

This year's vote for Trump's One Big Beautiful Bill suffered just three GOP "nays." Along with the lone Republican pair of "no" votes in the House of Representatives, that was enough for the $3.4 trillion bill to gain the president's signature. It gave big tax cuts to corporations and the wealthy while cutting health assistance to millions on Medicaid. But when President Trump lays down the law, Republican senators give no thought to either the next election or to the morality of the measure to which they've given their name.

....

Back in the fall of 1967, those of us on campus, especially those of draft age, watched the coming 1968 election with life-and-death interest. In October, I took part in the March on the Pentagon. This was the great antiwar protest that Norman Mailer would write about in *The Armies of the Night*.

That November, Senator Eugene McCarthy entered the presidential race. Suddenly President Johnson now had a candidate opposing his Vietnam War policies. Many college students quickly joined what was called his "children's crusade."

But Bobby Kennedy, the preferred antiwar candidate of "Dump Johnson" activist Allard K. Lowenstein, held back. The question weighing on Bobby was whether to run in 1968 against President Johnson or wait until LBJ vacated the White House in 1972. Kennedy feared that a run against LBJ would be seen as personal—not about his ideal of ending the Vietnam War, but rather as simply part of a personal feud. In a partisan country, he would also be toppling a Democratic president within a party that was itself deeply divided about the Vietnam War.

Two men argued strongly against a Kennedy challenge to the president. One, Ted Sorensen, who had been President Kennedy's speechwriter and the aide he called his "intellectual blood-bank." Two, Bobby's younger brother Ted, the senator from Massachusetts. Neither thought that Bobby should take the risk. Why not run when the coast was clear in 1972?

On the other side were the gung ho antiwar activists. *Village Voice* writer Jack Newfield weighed in with a powerful message. "If Kennedy does not run in 1968, the best side of his character will die."

Only after the stunning Tet Offensive by the North Vietnamese and the Vietcong showed the weakness of the government in Saigon did Kennedy make his final decision to run.

Another factor pushing Bobby to run was President Johnson's decision to totally ignore the findings of the Kerner Commission, the National Advisory Commission on Civil Disorders. It warned of America becoming "two societies, one black, one white—separate and unequal." It called for new jobs, new housing, and a new drive to end segregation. LBJ, despite having commissioned the group's report, paid no attention to it. Neither, consequentially, did the antiwar Eugene McCarthy. Bobby was determined to redirect the money going to the war to the problems of America's cities. Neither of his two potential rivals shared that goal.

Gene McCarthy went on to win 41.9 percent of the Democratic vote in the New Hampshire primary, threatening President Johnson and becoming an immediate hero of antiwar Americans.

The day before St. Patrick's Day, Bobby declared for president from the same Senate conference room where his brother had begun his campaign eight years before.

....

On July 4, 2025, President Donald Trump signed the Big Beautiful Bill. The legislation will add trillions to the national debt. Since then, the Trump administration has also proposed the repeal of the 2009 scientific finding that climate change endangers human health. Environmental Protection Agency administrator Lee Zeldin was downright gleeful. "This has been referred to as driving a dagger into the heart of the climate change religion," he said. But when will the Trump people defend America's young people against the dangers of climate change? Apparently, never.

A question for Democrats: You lost the 2024 presidential election over failure to secure the southern border. So what now? President Trump has deployed the National Guard to cut off illegal entry into the country. When will the Democrats offer their own plan to regulate immigration? Or will they allow the Republicans to continue accusing them of backing an "open border"? Failure to act simply keeps the "border" issue alive for the next election.

"Courage is the virtue that President Kennedy most admired," Bobby wrote in 1964, in his foreword to the memorial edition of *Profiles in Courage*. "He sought out those people who had demonstrated in some way, whether it was on a battlefield or a baseball diamond, in a speech or fighting for a cause, that they had courage, that they would stand up, that they could be counted on."

Unlike Gene McCarthy, Bobby had sacrificed something very real in 1968: the easy claim for the Democratic nomination in 1972. Once he declared against President Johnson he knew there would be no turning back.

3

Admit Your Mistakes

This country is run by people who never seem to make mistakes.

President Trump deems himself above reproach. "Apologizing's a great thing, but you have to be wrong. . . . I will absolutely apologize sometime in the hopefully distant future if I'm ever wrong." That statement comes from an interview Trump did with NBC's Jimmy Fallon in 2015.

He notoriously refused to offer the standard concession speech after losing the 2020 presidential election to Democrat Joe Biden. It was to "stop the steal" that he sent that mob to attack the US Capitol on January 6, 2021.

On refusing to admit error, Trump is hardly alone. Many leaders from both parties wildly backed the 2003 US invasion of Iraq. President George W. Bush took victory laps as our forces killed two hundred thousand Iraqi people. Yet no one confesses that it was all for nought. Do you hear W or Dick Cheney, his hawkish vice president, offering a syllable of confession?

Bobby Kennedy had a useful expression in this regard: *Hang a lantern on your problem.* To him it meant admitting your weakness before someone calls you on it.

....

Kennedy's confession of weakness concerned his failure to give much thought to civil rights. "I didn't lose much sleep over Negroes," he would say about his life before becoming US attorney general. "I didn't think about them much. I didn't know much about all the injustice." That was a remarkable admission given his later role in civil rights causes. He was talking about a basic lack of interest in this country's denial of rights to African Americans.

Apologies for misdeeds are not unheard-of. German Chancellor Willy Brandt, on a 1970 visit to Poland, knelt before a Warsaw Ghetto uprising monument. He was asking for forgiveness for the Holocaust itself.

Russian President Boris Yeltsin apologized for the Soviet attack on a Korean Air Lines flight in 1983 that killed all 269 on board, including US Congressman Larry McDonald. South African President F. W. de Klerk apologized in 1993 for apartheid, his government's system of white supremacy.

Closer to home, Alabama Governor George Wallace apologized for his segregationist views. "I was wrong. Those days are over, and they ought to be over." He asked for forgiveness from African Americans.

But will the Republicans in today's Congress ever apologize for their decision to kill the Voice of America? Will they be celebrating the growing influence of Chinese propaganda in the countries of South America, Africa, and Asia? As someone who loved listening to the VOA when I was a Peace Corps volunteer in Africa, I know its power. I'm not sure truth-telling will be the watchword of the People's Republic, which will take VOA's place in the developing world.

And when will the Democratic Party admit that it ran such a weak campaign for the presidency in 2024? The one that allowed Trump back into the White House?

By the way, what *was* Kamala Harris's border policy? Did she truly *intend* to match President Biden's "open border"? If not, why didn't she say so? And why did the Democrats campaign on cultural issues like abortion and LGBT rights, not on the economic issues that had the biggest impact on the voting electorate?

Despite his apologies about not caring about civil rights in his youth, Bobby deserves a historic credit in that department. As a law student at the University of Virginia, he headed the Student Legal Forum's lecture series. Among the guests he invited to the UVA campus was Dr. Ralph Bunche. Bunche had won the Nobel Peace Prize in 1950 for his leadership of the Israeli-Arab armistice negotiations. Bobby backed the Nobel laureate's demand that he speak to an integrated audience. "Ever since its inception the lectures sponsored by the Student Legal Forum have been open to the public at large," he wrote UVA president Colgate Darden. "At no time did it occur to us that it would be possible or desirable to have Dr. Bunche lecture under any other arrangement. There is no question but that Dr. Bunche will feel compelled to cancel his engagement if an educational segregation policy is invoked."

To win the argument, Bobby warned in his letter to President Darden that there could be Cold War consequences. By invoking a Jim Crow policy—this was Virginia in 1951—he said this could bring worldwide shame.

"The implications are obvious. At a time when the United States is battling a daily propaganda war with Russia, the racial issue would probably be spread across the headlines in its most damaging aspect. We believe the results would be catastrophic."

Bobby and Dr. Bunche prevailed. President Darden decided that, regardless of existing state law, UVA's distinguished visitor would speak to an integrated audience.

The night of the speech, Bunche stayed with the Kennedys. Ethel recalled that it was far from peaceful. "They threw things at the house all night," she told me.

But through the rest of the 1950s, Bobby admittedly showed little interest in the emerging civil rights movement. As his brother Jack's chief political operative, his goal was not so much to advance the struggle as to drive his brother's rise to the White House.

When Martin Luther King Jr. was arrested in Atlanta, Georgia, on the eve of the 1960 presidential election, for example, an aide had to go *around* Bobby to encourage the candidate, Jack Kennedy, to telephone his sympathy to Coretta Scott King. He dared not ask Bobby to take such a risk. Only later, when the injustice of the arrest had sunk in, did Bobby call the presiding judge and demand King's release.

All that indifference ended when Bobby became US attorney general. He did not become emotional about civil rights until his aide John Seigenthaler got his head hit with a pipe during a 1961 Freedom Ride.

Later, in the 1960s, when he came into conflict with President Johnson over the country's Vietnam policies, Kennedy offered another apology.

"Past error is no excuse for its own perpetration," Kennedy said. "We do ourselves best justice when we measure ourselves against ancient texts, as in Sophocles: 'All men make mistakes, but a good man yields when he knows his course is wrong, and he repairs the evil.'"

4

Pursue Ideals

After his brother's assassination in 1963, Bobby Kennedy took on a new agenda. He accepted the moral obligation of helping Mexican farmworkers and fighting Black suppression in South Africa. He was out to pursue his ideals.

The ideal of our current president is to idealize *himself*. He speaks of annexing Canada, buying Greenland, retaking the Panama Canal. He names friends and weekend Fox News stars to top positions and laughs at those who criticize his ambitions.

Meanwhile, the president denigrates American heroes. In 2018, he canceled a visit to the American military cemetery at Aisne-Marne. He called the World War I soldiers buried in the French cemetery "losers" and "suckers" for getting killed in battle. Retired Marine Corps General John Kelly, then Trump's chief of staff, confirmed that he heard Trump's very words. On a trip through Arlington National Cemetery, Trump was passing by the grave of Robert Kelly, the general's son. The younger Kelly had been killed fighting in Afghanistan. "I don't get it. What was in it for them?" Trump said, referring to Robert Kelly and other marines who lost their lives in defense of country.

But isn't that what patriotic duty sometimes involves? This country came back from World War II confident of our morality, knowing we took the noble course. We had defeated Adolf Hitler and were stronger for it. We fed the poor of the world; we encouraged democracy. In a larger sense, isn't this the moral certitude we need as a country? Isn't this what we're longing for today?

....

Toward the end of Bobby's life, Jack Newfield wrote, "Bobby Kennedy was filled with a new resolution, a new commitment to the downtrodden, whether they are migrant farm workers organizing with Cesar Chavez, native Americans battling poverty and alcoholism, poor Blacks or working-class Whites."

In March 1965, Bobby flew to California to meet with Cesar Chavez, who was leading the migrant workers' strike against the grape growers. Bobby's attitude soon switched from lack of interest—"Why are we making this trip?"—to full engagement.

He became outraged on hearing about the arrests of dozens of picketing workers. A local sheriff, loyal to the farm owners, said that the workers had been arrested because they were "*ready* to violate the law." *Ready?* Bobby suggested "that the sheriff and the district attorney read the Constitution of the United States." It would show, he said, that a sheriff cannot arrest someone because they thought them "ready" to commit a crime.

Chavez, whose role models were Gandhi and Martin Luther King Jr., soon saw Bobby as a champion for his cause. "He crossed a line that no other American politician ever crossed," Chavez told Jack Newfield.

It was more than Kennedy's political courage, his readiness to side with the farmworkers against the powerful owners. What really grabbed Chavez was his authenticity. More than that, it was Bobby's growth as a human being, his willingness to become someone better through experience.

"In the twelve years which ensued I watched the development of a man into the ablest and most compassionate leader this country has ever developed," JFK press secretary Pierre Salinger wrote.

He continued, "When I first met Bob he saw the world in rather simple black-and-white terms. His real growth was his ability to grasp the complexities of our modern world and to be able to understand the shades of gray which abound in the problems we face. He never compromised with principle, but the maturing Bob Kennedy was able to see and understand the adversary's position."

In June 1966, Bobby traveled to Cape Town to speak to thousands of young white students. His topic, though he didn't address it directly, was apartheid.

He made a point not to judge South African whites but pointed to the common history of our two lands.

> I come here . . . because of my deep interest and affection for a land settled by the Dutch in the mid-seventeenth century, then taken over by the British, and at last independent; a land in which the native inhabitants were at first subdued, but relations with whom remain a problem to this day; a land which defined itself on a hostile frontier; a land which has tamed rich natural resources through the energetic application of modern technology; a land which was once the importer of slaves, and now must struggle to wipe out the last traces of that former bondage.

After a pause, he continued. "I refer, of course, to the United States of America."

He added, "Nations, like men, often march to the beat of different drummers, and the precise solutions of the United States can neither be dictated nor transplanted to others."

Bobby then offered the young South Africans a personal goal that each and every one of them might adopt: to accept "the full human equality of all of our people" and "wipe away the unnecessary sufferings of our fellow human beings." He said that we cannot "cling to a present which is already dying" and that opposes "even the most peaceful progress."

The hopes of the world, he concluded, lie with our young people.

He spoke of "the danger of futility; the belief there is nothing one man or one woman can do against the enormous array of the world's ills." At the age of thirty-three, he said, Thomas Jefferson "proclaimed that all men are created equal."

He continued:

> It is from numberless diverse acts of courage . . . that human history is thus shaped. Each time a man stands up for an ideal, or acts to improve the lot of others, or strikes out against injustice, he sends forth a tiny ripple of hope, and crossing each other from a million different centers of energy and daring, those ripples build a current which can sweep down the mightiest walls of oppression and resistance.

I worry about our country's direction. I refer to the government but also to the weakened opposition; we are divided and adrift. But we still have the instinct to spot the bully on the playground. We can *feel* the difference between right and wrong. So, can the United States again be the world leader and valiant ally we grew up believing ourselves to be? Are we ready and willing to once again be the world's good guy?

5

Uphold Human Rights

In 1963, Martin Luther King Jr. decided to challenge Jim Crow in Birmingham, Alabama. It was a city where jobs, restaurants, and restrooms were then governed by strict segregation. Dr. King believed it was a city ready to have its brutal suppression of African Americans exposed to the country.

In May, hundreds of students marched through the city without a permit. They went face-to-face with local police, who were under the command of Eugene "Bull" Connor, the city's commissioner of public safety. Connor responded with high-pressure fire hoses and police dogs. Terrified, the young people stood their ground, singing as armed men with billy clubs bore down on them.

Americans around the country, watching TV in their living rooms, could now see the horror of peaceful protesters risking their lives to fight Jim Crow. One camera caught a police dog sinking its teeth into the chest of one of the students.

Thanks to Bobby Kennedy's Justice Department, all those arrested schoolchildren were released from jail. Segregation in Birmingham ended in ninety days.

Presidents should build on such rights of citizenship. This administration has instead tried to shrink them.

Start with the most American of freedoms, the right to vote.

Donald Trump says he won the 2020 presidential election—that he was never defeated for reelection. His inability to win that argument continues.

To triumph in the most contested states, the MAGA forces carry on a fight to change their laws. According to the Brennan Center for Justice, they include: limiting mail-in voting, toughening ID requirements, and stopping early voting and same-day registration. The goal is to restrict voting overall, but especially among racial minorities.

....

Bobby Kennedy knew that the outcome in Birmingham in 1963, while successful, had raised a storm among white Southerners. To help brave it, he asked author James Baldwin to bring a group of activists to the Kennedy family's apartment in New York. They included Harry Belafonte; Lorraine

Hansberry, who wrote *A Raisin in the Sun*; and psychologist Kenneth Clark, whose work with Black youth had aided in the Supreme Court's *Brown vs. Board of Education* decision that banned racial segregation in US public schools.

At the gathering, the heat rose quickly, especially for Bobby himself, when a young civil rights advocate, one of the original Freedom Riders, said he would not accept service in the Vietnam War. "What you're asking us young Black people to do is pick up guns against people in Asia while you have continued to deny us our rights." The next time the police used fire hoses and dogs on him and his fellow protesters, he promised to respond with a gun.

Hearing this, and watching Bobby's angry reaction, Hansberry said it was the young Freedom Rider that Bobby should be listening to, not the older, more moderate African Americans in the room. Adding her voice, the singer Lena Horne said: "He communicated the plain, basic suffering of being a Negro." Such brutal encounters had an effect. By the time of his death, John Lewis said, Kennedy's attitude had changed from concern about the political fallout of the Freedom Riders to an identification "with the new and moving force within the Black community and the civil rights movement."

On hearing Hansberry's account of the New York meeting, Martin Luther King Jr. was impressed. "Maybe it's what Bobby needed to hear. He's going to hear a lot more of it if the president keeps dawdling on that civil rights bill."

Bobby's own reaction, after he recovered from the verbal assault, was: "I guess if I were in his shoes, I might feel differently about this country."

To Arthur Schlesinger, the meeting and Bobby's reaction to it meant "a much stronger civil rights bill this session than anyone had previously contemplated."

Paul Corbin, a Kennedy confidant, had become exasperated by Bobby's abstract thinking about civil rights. He didn't seem to get it. He once asked Bobby what he would *feel* like if he had to drive around the South, going from gas station to gas station, asking if his wife could, in Paul's words, "take a piss."

Pierre Salinger saw Bobby take Corbin's way of thinking to heart. "He could not stand the idea that other people suffered. When he talked of hunger and deprivation—he did not cite statistics—he talked in terms of human beings he had seen. He wanted so much to ease suffering and injustice—he had such genuine compassion—that it almost became an obsession with him. The dispossessed understood that, and that's why they believed him."

Driven by the events in Birmingham, the Kennedys now had to settle with George Wallace, who had promised "segregation now, segregation tomorrow, segregation forever."

Wallace, even after Birmingham, was determined to fight a court order to admit two African American students to the University of Alabama in Tuscaloosa. He promised to "stand in the schoolhouse door" to prevent it.

Crisis, a Robert Drew documentary, shows what occurred in the Oval Office on June 11, 1963, shortly after Kennedy saw TV coverage of the events in Tuscaloosa. "I think we'd better give that speech tonight," the president said, referring to an address on civil rights that was already in the works.

With Ted Sorensen and Bobby working on the text right up to its delivery, President Kennedy spoke to the nation: "I hope that every American, regardless of where he lives, will stop and examine his conscience. . . . This Nation was founded by men of many nations and backgrounds. It was founded on the principle that all men are created equal, and that the rights of every man are diminished when the rights of one man are threatened."

What America faced, Kennedy argued, was a "moral" crisis. "It is as old as the scriptures and is as clear as the American Constitution."

Bobby Kennedy pushed his brother to make that first-ever presidential declaration for civil rights and to make it on television.

"He urged it, he felt it, he understood it. And he prevailed," Assistant Attorney General Burke Marshall said later.

"Every single person who spoke about it in the White House—every one of them—was against President Kennedy sending up that bill, against his speech in June, against making it a moral issue. . . . I don't think there was anybody in the Cabinet—except the President himself—who felt that way on these issues, and the President got it from his brother," Marshall said.

Harris Wofford, the White House advisor on civil rights and later a United States senator, agreed. "Kennedy thought the moment was right to go beyond anything he had said as President, and to ask the country and Congress to go beyond anything it had done since Reconstruction."

....

Martin Luther King Jr. called Kennedy's June 1963 speech "the most sweeping and forthright ever presented by an American president." King is elsewhere reported to have said, "Can you believe that white man not only stepped up to the plate, he hit it over the fence!"

We need to think a bit longer about that address. The call for civil rights was made on moral ground. Kennedy asked that we examine our conscience. He was taking us not just to the Founding Fathers but to the "scriptures," to the Bible itself.

But that night's talk from the Oval Office was also about basic human decency, how each of us would like to be treated ourselves. It was about facing daily the oppressive rules of Jim Crow—about being a young boy or girl in the streets facing police fire hoses and the gnashing dogs of Bull Connor.

6

Seek Peace

We live in a world of nuclear powers. The United States, France, the United Kingdom, Russia, China, North Korea, India, Pakistan, and Israel all have the bomb. Iran is clearly dying to get one.

The goal for the United States is to limit the number of countries that possess nuclear weapons and therefore the danger this proliferation poses. By attacking Iranian nuclear sites with B-2 stealth bombers in June 2025, President Trump hoped to set back that country's production of nuclear weapons.

But by jeopardizing our relations with the North Atlantic Treaty Organization (NATO), the president may have encouraged its member nations to go it alone and develop their own nuclear arsenals. Without the guarantee of the American nuclear "umbrella," NATO countries could decide they've been put in jeopardy.

Again, it's a case where the Bobby Kennedy of history matters. In 1962, the last time the US and Russia faced each other with nuclear weapons, he played a critical peacekeeping role.

That crisis, the Cuban Missile Crisis, had begun a year earlier with the failed US-supported invasion at the Bay of Pigs. Bobby had no part in planning or approving the invasion in the spring of 1961. But following this disastrous attempt by Cuban expatriates to reclaim their island nation from Fidel Castro's Communist regime, President Kennedy never made another move without him.

Here's Lyndon Johnson, a vice president forever wary of Robert Kennedy, on Bobby's role in the New Frontier: "Every time they have a conference don't tell me about who is the top advisor. It isn't [Defense Secretary] McNamara, the chiefs of staff, or anybody else like that. Bobby is first in, last out. And Bobby is the boy he *listens* to."

He is also a US leader who knew how to face—and avoid—a nuclear confrontation.

Following the failed Bay of Pigs invasion, Bobby warned that the Soviets would soon bring nuclear weapons to Cuba. He assumed that the USSR would do this for no other reason than to prevent an even stronger US attack on Russia's island ally.

On October 15, 1962, Bobby's prediction had come true. A U-2 reconnaissance flight discovered three ballistic missile launch sites in Cuba. It was determined that the missiles held there were medium-range, capable of reaching targets 1,100 miles away. That made Washington itself a potential target.

On being briefed, Bobby responded with a single word: "Shit!"

Both Kennedys understood the stakes, that the true nuclear challenge lay in Europe. Nikita Khrushchev had said that any US attack on Cuba would mean Russian tanks advancing on US-occupied West Berlin.

The failure to act also carried risks. The world remembered the 1938 Munich Conference, where the British and French sold out Czechoslovakia to Hitler.

At first, Bobby was a real "hawk," calling for a quick air strike. He had predicted the Soviets would pull this, and he was well prepared to meet the Communist threat and "take our losses." Robert McNamara saw him as the most aggressive of the president's advisors.

Yet as the days passed, both Jack and Bobby found themselves moving from hawk to dove. They believed the swift air strike and the likelihood of Russian casualties risked a Soviet countermove toward West Berlin. Given the Warsaw Pact's advantage in tanks and men, a conflict at the border could rapidly lead to a nuclear standoff.

For this reason, the Kennedys decided on a blockade. Bobby set out the moral rationale. "For 175 years we had not been that kind of country. A sneak attack was not in our tradition. Thousands of Cubans would be killed without warning, and a lot of Russians too." He wanted the Soviets to know we were serious but he also wanted to allow them room to pull back.

With the clock running, Jack asked Bobby to meet Ambassador Anatoly Dobrynin at the Justice Department with a secret US offer. Bobby was to tell Dobrynin that the American president didn't know how long he could call off his hawks.

Dobrynin delivered Bobby's words to the Kremlin. He had seen that the attorney general was nothing like himself that evening. There was none of his usual aggressiveness. On the contrary, he was visibly upset, worried like any other parent about the world's children. "I should say that during that meeting R. Kennedy was very upset. I've never seen him like this before." He relayed the president's concerns about the generals "itching for a fight." Kennedy told Dobrynin that the United States would agree to no further attempts to invade Cuba and also secretly agreed to meet a second Soviet demand to remove American nuclear missiles from Turkey and Italy within five months.

The response from Khrushchev was positive. "To save the world," the Soviet chairman declared, "we must retreat."

And that was it. The USSR removed its missiles from Cuba, and a nuclear war was avoided. The communications had all been through government channels. But then Dobrynin stopped by with a personal note from Nikita Khrushchev himself. He "wanted to send his good wishes to both Kennedys."

The result of that goodwill, reached in August 1963, was the Partial Nuclear Test Ban Treaty, signed by the United States, the Soviet Union, and the United Kingdom.

One of the great truths of the Cold War is how the very existence of nuclear weapons kept the United States from entering a third world war. But that only holds true in 2025 because *all* of the nuclear powers know the horrors. The longer the list of nuclear powers, the greater the chance that one leader does not. This remains a cataclysm we must find some way to avoid.

7

Enforce the Law

Donald Trump entered the White House on January 20, 2025, with high personal ambition. He issued executive orders dismantling all forms of diversity, equity, and inclusion. He wanted to expand this elimination of DEI beyond the federal government to every college and corporation.

Bobby Kennedy began his career at the Justice Department with the opposite ambition. His job, which he pursued with a personal passion, was to *enforce* federal court orders to end racial segregation in state universities.

He had a second ambition, largely unspoken: to explain to young Justice Department lawyers why he was named US attorney general at age thirty-five with no courtroom experience.

So here he was sharing with the other young prosecutors the image of his brother, the president-elect, standing in front of his

Georgetown house. It had come time for his older brother to announce the appointment of his attorney general.

"Jack told me to go upstairs and comb my hair, to which I said it was the first time the president had ever told the attorney general to comb his hair before they made the announcement."

Knowing how it would come across, Bobby then went into the details of his rise to being such a young attorney general.

"I started in the Department as a young lawyer in 1950. The salary was only $4,000 a year, but I worked hard. I was ambitious. I studied. I applied myself. And then my brother was elected president of the United States."

That was Bobby's way of admitting the obvious charge of nepotism. His confession of reality was his way of *hanging a lantern on his problem*. He had not been in an actual courtroom in his life. But it's also, looking back, one of the great cabinet appointments on record. Today the Justice Department is housed in what is called the Robert F. Kennedy Building, and for good reason.

....

In May 1961, the first of the Freedom Riders headed from Washington to the Deep South. Their goal was to test a recent Supreme Court decision that outlawed discrimination on interstate buses.

When the new attorney general heard of the Freedom Riders, his impulse was to shut them down. An angry mob had already attacked them as they entered Alabama. Passengers fleeing one bus were beaten with baseball bats. Those on the bus that had reached Birmingham were slammed with iron pipes and bicycle chains.

"Stop them!" Bobby instructed civil rights advisor Harris Wofford. "Get your friends off those buses."

Kennedy's fears connected directly with the Cold War. His brother, the president, was about to meet with Soviet leader Nikita Khrushchev in Vienna. The United States had just gone through the Bay of Pigs disaster. Bobby did not want a major racial protest in the United States to add to the USSR propaganda.

To monitor the Freedom Riders, Bobby then sent John Seigenthaler, his administrative assistant, to follow the buses. When Seigenthaler got to the Montgomery, Alabama, bus station, he heard screams and knew already there was trouble. He leaped from his car only to have two men grab hold of him.

"Get back!" he shouted. "I'm from the federal government." It was then, as he turned away from the men, that he was struck on the head. He lay on the ground for about a half hour before the local police picked him up and took him to the hospital.

That slam against John Seigenthaler's head got the attorney general's attention *personally*. "Robert Kennedy became educated in a real hurry," recalled Freedom Rider John Lewis, the future Georgia US congressman. "And I can tell you the thing that sealed it for him, perhaps more than anything else—after John Seigenthaler was beaten, someone he knew."

Seigenthaler himself said, "I think everything he thought the administration of justice and law enforcement was supposed to be about had been violated . . . and that it was an outrage, a stain on law enforcement that we let that happen."

Bobby Kennedy saw the way local police treated a federal official and it got to him emotionally. Civil rights advocate Harry Belafonte also noticed. "At last, Bobby's moral center seemed to stir." The attorney general went on the Voice of America just days after the rioting at the Montgomery bus station. He told how what happened to Seigenthaler in Alabama got to the core of his beliefs about justice. It reminded him of how his own Irish family had been treated so nastily when they first arrived here.

He tried to find hope in the country's history. "Now an Irish Catholic is president of the United States. There is no question about it—in the next forty years, a Negro can achieve the same position my brother did.

With the election of Barack Obama in 2008, Bobby's prediction was just seven years off.

....

Shortly after John F. Kennedy's inaugural, James Meredith, a Black air force veteran, applied for admission to the University of Mississippi in Oxford. Knowing how Ole Miss used endless "delaying tactics" to effectively ban African Americans, he twice wrote to the Justice Department. He said he was inspired to do so in each case by John F. Kennedy's election as president.

"What do I want from you?" he asked the department. "I think that the power and influence of the federal government should be used" to get him what he was entitled to. "I simply ask that the federal agencies use the power and prestige of their positions to ensure the full rights of citizenship for our people."

Mississippi Governor Ross Barnett already had his reply. "I won't agree to let that boy go to Ole Miss," he told the attorney general.

Barnett told Kennedy to go ahead and send in the US Army to overwhelm the local police. But Bobby could see that the governor was constructing another Theater of the Lost Cause. He wanted the historic incident to be yet another re-enactment of the Civil War, of federal troops forcing the people of Mississippi into submission.

Bobby chose a simpler way to get James Meredith into Ole Miss. He decided to get him to the campus on a Sunday, accompanied by US marshals and two aides from the Department of Justice, and to have him register on Monday.

Even this caused a ruckus. Ed Guthman, one of the DOJ aides, himself a Pulitzer Prize–winning reporter, who Bobby had sent to the scene, told the attorney general about the size and anger of the mob around him. He said it was "like the Alamo." Alarmed that Meredith might get hurt, Bobby ordered, "Shoot anybody that puts a hand on him."

Hearing about that night in Oxford, the heat and anger of that crowd at Ole Miss, brought Bobby to a new awareness of the depth of opposition to racial integration in the Deep South.

Federal court orders need to be accepted. This is essential to the balance among our three branches of government. Once the appeals have run their course, the US attorney general has no choice in the matter. In insisting on James Meredith's admission to Ole Miss, Kennedy was acting admirably. But it was also the *moral* course.

8

Be Tough

The greatest principle of Bobby Kennedy's life was *personal responsibility*. He felt compassion for poor Americans, white and Black alike. But he insisted that people obey the law.

The attorney general was a liberal of a different type: a *tough* liberal.

Unlike his brother, the cool JFK, he grappled soul to soul with the passions of the sixties and its revolutions. It was Bobby who put his heart, mind, and guts into those struggles.

But he was no bleeding heart. Personal tragedy and some hard political lessons had made him of stronger stuff. He managed to combine a passion for social justice with a strong dedication to the duties that must face all citizens.

On the evening after Martin Luther King Jr.'s assassination, Bobby was scheduled to speak in an African American neighborhood in Indianapolis. Civil rights leader John Lewis organized that evening's event. "There were some people saying that maybe he shouldn't come, because maybe there would be violence. But some of us said he *must* come." Lewis was one of them.

The candidate himself agreed. "Our local campaign leadership, and the city leaders, urged that the meeting be canceled, because security could not be guaranteed," Frank Mankiewicz recalled. "But Kennedy insisted that was one of the reasons he had to keep the date."

The local police refused to join the Kennedy motorcade as it entered the rally site. "What am I going to say?" Bobby asked his aides as they drove past the crowded sidewalks. When he reached the microphone, Kennedy wondered openly if the crowd knew that Dr. King had just been killed. "Do they know about Martin Luther King?" you can hear him ask his hosts. They hadn't.

"I have some very sad news for all of you," he began. "And that is that Martin Luther King was shot and was killed tonight in Memphis, Tennessee."

There was a collective gasp. At first, the listeners didn't believe what they were hearing. There was even scattered applause from those simply excited that Bobby Kennedy was there among them. Only then did they begin to make out his words.

He continued:

Martin Luther King dedicated his life to love and to justice between fellow human beings. He died in the cause of that effort.

In this difficult day, in this difficult time for the United States, it's perhaps well to ask what kind of a nation we are, and what direction we want to move in.

For those of you who are black—considering the evidence evidently is that there were white people who were responsible—you can be filled with bitterness, and with hatred, and a desire for revenge. We can move in that direction as a country, in greater polarization . . . filled with hatred toward one another.

Or we can make an effort, as Martin Luther King did, to understand and . . . replace that violence, that stain of bloodshed that has spread across our land, with an effort to understand, with compassion, and love.

For those of you who are black and are tempted to be filled with hatred and mistrust of the injustice of such an act, against all white people, I would only say that . . . I had a member of my family killed—but he was killed by a white man. But we have to make an effort in the United States. We have to make an effort to understand, to get beyond or go beyond these rather difficult times.

Finally:

> What we need in the United States is not division. What we need in the United States is not hatred. What we need in the United States is not violence and lawlessness, but love and wisdom, and compassion toward one another, a feeling of justice toward those who still suffer within our country—whether they be white or whether they be black.
>
> We can do well in this country. We will have difficult times. We've had difficult times in the past. We will have difficult times in the future. It is not the end of violence. It is not the end of lawlessness, and it is not the end of disorder. . . .
>
> Let us dedicate ourselves to what the Greeks wrote so many years ago: to tame the savageness of man and make gentle the life of this world.
>
> Let us dedicate ourselves to that, and say a prayer for our country and for our people. Thank you very much.

That reference to a "member of my family" was the sole public mention he ever made regarding his relationship to what he would call "the events of November 1963."

Speaking to the Cleveland City Club the next day, Kennedy

said that the angry African Americans now in the streets were not the only perpetrators of violence:

> No one—no matter where he lives or what he does—can be certain who will suffer from some senseless act of bloodshed. And yet it goes on and on. . . . Whenever any American's life is taken by another American unnecessarily—whether it is done in the name of the law or in the defiance of the law, by one man or a gang, in cold blood or in passion, in an attack of violence or in response to violence; whenever we tear at the fabric of life which another man has painfully and clumsily woven for himself and his children, the whole nation is degraded. . . .
>
> There is another kind of violence, slower but just as deadly, destructive as the shot or the bomb in the night. This is the violence of institutions; indifference and inaction and slow decay. This is the violence that afflicts the poor, that poisons relations between men because their skin has different colors. This is a slow destruction of a child by hunger, and schools without books and homes without heat in the winter.
>
> This is the breaking of a man's spirit by denying him the chance to stand as a father and as a man among other men. And this too afflicts us all. I have not come

> here to propose a set of specific remedies nor is there a single set. For a broad and adequate outline we know what must be done. When you teach a man to hate and fear his brother, when you teach that he is a lesser man because of his color or his beliefs or the policies he pursues, when you teach that those who differ from you threaten your freedom or your job or your family, then you also learn to confront others not as fellow citizens but as enemies—to be met not with cooperation but with conquest, to be subjugated and mastered.
>
> We learn, at the last, to look at our brothers as aliens, men with whom we share a city, but not a community, men bound to us in common dwelling, but not in common effort. We learn to share only a common fear—only a common desire to retreat from each other—only a common impulse to meet disagreement with force.

....

Though he was a man of compassion, Bobby believed in law and order and didn't hesitate to use that precise phrase. He fought discrimination, despaired over the shooting of Dr. King, but was unable to tolerate watching the streets of the nation's capital being burned in protest.

"I think ingrained at the very core of his character was a

sense that you have to have a lawful society if you're going to have a peaceful society," said Justice Department aide John Seigenthaler. "He just thought that liberalism didn't have a chance to work where you have crime and violence."

His daughter Kerry Kennedy, just eight years old in April 1968, recalled sitting with her father in their Virginia home. It was in those days just after Dr. King's killing. They were watching on television as Washington burned. She remembers her dad saying that it was bad for people to "loot and destroy," even though he understood the frustration and anger that those in the streets felt.

What would Bobby Kennedy think had he seen the mob that attacked the US Capitol on January 6, 2021? Watching people shoving flagpoles through doors and into the bodies of Capitol Police officers? What would he think of an American president sitting in the White House watching all this on television and doing nothing? Watching even as the mob searched for Vice President Mike Pence? Or of this American president who later *pardons* those caught committing violent crimes against our democracy?

9

Know When to Concede

Donald Trump refused to concede the 2020 presidential election. He refused to halt the January 6 "Stop the Steal" attack on the US Capitol. He refused to attend the inauguration of Joe Biden on January 20, 2021.

This may have been Trump's worst crime against the American constitutional system. It definitely gets to the heart of it. The honest transfer of presidential authority is one of this country's highest traditions. American citizens are proud to have elections that are carried out honestly, and proud to have this transfer of power seen by the world. I think of all the concession speeches in my life: Jimmy Carter, Walter Mondale, George H. W. Bush, Bob Dole, Al Gore (after the long recount), John Kerry, John McCain, Mitt Romney, Hillary Clinton, and Kamala Harris. In his selfish interest, Donald Trump chose to undercut that tradition.

....

Here's a rule. Don't run for office if you're incapable of telling the truth about the results. Again, Bobby Kennedy offers the perfect model.

Weeks before his death, Robert Kennedy could already see himself losing the Oregon presidential primary. The strongest reason had been his own delay in entering the race. Eugene McCarthy offered his anti–Vietnam War challenge in November 1967. Bobby Kennedy had waited until March. He could see himself about to be punished by Oregon's antiwar Democrats.

I recall watching Roger Mudd of CBS News interview Kennedy in an airport. When the newsman asked him if it bothered him that so many college students had stuck with McCarthy, the look on his face told us the answer. *Boston Globe* reporter Robert Healy said that really "gnawed" at Bobby.

Another problem, close to home, was his lack of a gifted campaign manager, someone whose work would match what he himself had done for his brother Jack in 1960. It meant that his campaign was unable to change direction quickly as it needed to in Oregon.

But on some issues Bobby didn't want to change course. "This just may not be my time," he admitted. He was doing what he wanted to be doing. He was talking about the people in the cities and about their problems. Some of his advisors told him that the problems of the cities were remote to the voters of Oregon and might cost him votes in the primary if he did not change.

Just a week before his death, he lost the Oregon presidential primary. It was the first time Bobby had lost an election, either as Jack Kennedy's campaign manager or as a candidate himself.

Columnist Jules Witcover described him "in his shirtsleeves, tie off but still wearing the PT-109 tie clasp that had been the symbol of Kennedy political invincibility. He had a heavily watered-down drink in his hand, and he was in a quiet, reflective mood—not bitter, not shocked, not even transparently disappointed, just resigned."

Bobby said that he could sense days before the Oregon primary that he was in trouble when he failed to get a responsive reaction from Portland factory workers. He could tell, he said, that they weren't tuned in, that he wasn't communicating with them. He asked aides where he had run well and where poorly, and he took the information much like the campaign manager he once was. One reporter asked him if he thought Oregon had hurt him, and it made him laugh. "It certainly wasn't one of the more helpful developments of the day," he said.

But he refused to blame his campaigners. "If I'd won it, it would have been my victory, and I've lost it and it's my defeat. I sometimes wonder if I've correctly sensed the mood of America. I think I have. But maybe I'm all wrong. Maybe the people don't want things changed. I do better with people who have problems."

Pat Buchanan, then a campaign researcher for Richard Nixon, was impressed by the way Kennedy absorbed the shock of losing. "His graciousness in conceding defeat and congratulating Gene McCarthy was impressive. This is the first time I'd seen Bobby in person. He could not have shown himself better in victory than he did in defeat that night."

"I can accept the fact I may not be nominated now," Bobby told Jack Newfield. "If that happens, I will just go back to the Senate, and say what I believe, and not try again in '72. Somebody has to speak up for the Negroes, and Indians, and Mexicans, and poor whites. Maybe that's what I do best. Maybe my personality just isn't built for this. . . . The issues are more important than me now."

Looking forward to the California primary, Bobby raised the stakes.

First, he agreed to meet Gene McCarthy in a nationally televised debate. "I'm not in much of a position now to say he's not a serious candidate. Hell, if he's not a serious candidate after tonight, then I'm not a candidate at all."

Second, he promised to end his campaign if he lost in California.

The honest acceptance of his loss in Oregon showed that Kennedy wasn't the "ruthless" figure he'd been called.

....

Bobby Kennedy matters because he acknowledged defeat. That is the enduring reality here. If the loser in an election refuses to offer a public, televised concession speech, he is sharing his denial with his followers. That's what Donald Trump, the loser of the 2020 presidential election, told his MAGA crowd as they headed to the US Capitol on January 6, 2021.

I have long taken pride that we as Americans participate in a vibrant democracy—living in a country where those who lose elections give a public accounting of their loss. They don't blame the count; they don't blame the democratic system itself.

....

I recall sitting in our basement rec room with Dad watching the 1958 midterm election results. New York Governor Averell Harriman came on to offer his concession speech. He'd just lost the race to Nelson Rockefeller. My father felt an immediate emotional connection with the governor's loss. As a middle-class guy, he could nonetheless identify personally with the moment the fabulously wealthy Harriman was facing.

That was my introduction to watching national election results and to truly understanding our democracy. For years, through election after election, I have looked forward to the concession speech. It is a bittersweet time for those who fought hard in a campaign, especially for the candidate who just learned he or she had lost.

But it is a clear sign that the campaign is *over.* All the TV ads and bumper stickers have done their business. Now we saw that the people have had their say. The winner has been decided. The loser has just told us so. It brings a crackling reality to the whole exercise. Our great democracy has won again.

I especially took pride in our free and open democratic system when I served in the Peace Corps. As I hitchhiked my way up through East Africa, I saw young democracies where the losers would predictably claim that the election had been stolen. I have also personally witnessed a good number of elections in my career. I lost a primary myself running for Congress in 1974. I saw my first boss, Senator Frank Moss, lose his reelection bid in Utah two years later and in 1980 watched my boss Jimmy Carter go down. In both those cases, the losing candidates, *my* candidates, gave public concession speeches.

Yet on January 6, we saw the same cheap charges—"Stop the Steal"—being thrown here in the United States.

President Trump, defeated in the November 2020 election by seven million votes in the popular count, told a crowd of unruly supporters to head to the Capitol. Once there, they tore through the doors and left a trail of mayhem. It took the combined US Capitol and Metropolitan Police to stop them before they could bring real harm or worse to members of Congress and to Trump's own vice president.

10

Sacrifice

People who run for high office must face risks.

Bobby Kennedy certainly did when he campaigned with such physical confidence in the 1968 California primary. It is one of the things that singled him out as a great public figure. It is also the way he died. Born into a world of affluence, patriotism, and power, he grew up with cardinals, movie stars, diplomats, and financiers, but he would be killed reaching out for the hand of a Mexican American busboy who earned $75 a week.

Arthur Schlesinger recalled a comment Jacqueline Kennedy made in the spring of that fateful year. Taking him aside one evening, she said, "Do you know what I think will happen to Bobby?"

When Schlesinger failed to offer a ready response, Jacqueline said, "The same thing that happened to Jack. . . .

There is so much hatred in the country, and more people hate Bobby than hated Jack. . . . I've told Bobby this, but he isn't fatalistic, like me."

Here is what the historian wrote himself about Bobby's own thinking: "He went through this all with his sense of fatality. Perhaps no one would have been less surprised than Robert Kennedy himself by the tragic conclusion of his life. He was vividly aware of the interior tensions of American society."

Americans watch each day as the US Senate bows to President Trump. He supports tariffs, which raise the cost of living. They kneel in obedience. He punishes historic wartime allies like Canada and democratic Europe. They kneel again. He pardons criminals, including the attackers on the Capitol itself; they worship the injustice.

....

Bobby Kennedy showed us the courage we should expect from US senators and other public servants.

By the middle of May 1968, he was getting more and more death threats. Refusing to think about his own safety, he showed a fatalism about his electoral chances.

"Perhaps we can accomplish something." He talked frequently of "bringing the country back together," of what we can achieve with "all of us working together."

"If the division continues, we're going to have nothing but chaos and havoc here in the United States. I think we can end the divisions within the United States, whether it's between blacks and whites, between the poor and the more affluent or between age groups or on the war in Vietnam. We can start to work together. We are a great country, an unselfish country. I intend to make that my basis for running."

And then on June 5, in the early-morning hours just after his victory in the California primary, the shots were fired. As he lay mortally wounded, his last words were: "Is everyone all right?"

We need men and women of courage, those able to run for public office unafraid that they might be primaried in the next election.

Bobby entered the 1968 presidential campaign despite the obvious risks to his political career. He did so even though those closest to him, including his brother Ted, warned him that it would ruin his chances of being easily nominated and elected once Lyndon Johnson left office.

The year 1968 held high stakes for this country. John Kennedy had been killed; now Martin Luther King Jr. was dead. But civil rights leader John Lewis could say "we still have Bobby."

When Bobby Kennedy died on June 6, there arose none of the pageantry we recall from President Kennedy's funeral. There were no marching bands, there was no music, no drumbeat, and certainly none of the "terrible beauty" poetry of William Butler Yeats.

When Robert Francis Kennedy was carried in the dark to the gravesite on the sloping hill in Arlington National Cemetery near his brother, it was only about loss.

His presidential campaign had lasted eighty-two days. He knew the odds against him. Conscience, not glory, was what had called Bobby to this "honorable adventure," a phrase he quoted in a new foreword to *Profiles in Courage*. He wanted to end the Vietnam War. He wanted to improve the lives of the country's poor, white and Black. But his death left a void as large as his promise.

"God bless you, RFK" and "We love you Bobby," read the hand-painted signs carried by people along the train tracks. That was the message as he left us.

Today, a hundred years after his birth, we need this kind of leader. The hope he offered and the message he bore are more important than ever. It's hard to find a liberal as tough as Kennedy was on law enforcement or a conservative anywhere near as committed to social justice.

But as that campaign moved on to California, Bobby faced danger, and not simply of a second primary defeat. Rather, mortal danger. Why does that matter in 2025? It matters because hatred can be provoked more easily today than it was in 1968.

....

"From the minute I met him," Bobby's Senate aide Adam Walinsky told me, "he was the most open-minded, most sensitive, feeling person I ever met who had anything to do with power."

But his real funeral service was in the eyes of the wounded faces alongside the tracks as the train made its way to Arlington and to his beloved older brother.

Here's what Ted Kennedy said of the people's response to Bobby's death:

> But most of all, it has been the people, the people themselves, with outstretched hands of sympathy and strength that have most touched the hearts of the members of my family. It is the ones who could give the least who have given the most.
>
> In the thousands who filed through St. Patrick's and stood on the streets of New York and stood on the railroad embankment.

Lastly came Arthur Schlesinger's comparison of Jack and Bobby:

> JFK attacked conditions because they seemed irrational, RFK because they seemed hateful. JFK was a man of cerebration; Bobby was very bright and reflective, but

> he was a man of commitment. If JFK saw people living in squalor, it seemed to him totally unreasonable and awful, but he saw it all, as FDR would have done, from the outside. RFK had an astonishing capacity to identify himself with the casualties and victims of our society. When he went among them, these were his children, his scraps of food, his hovels. JFK was urbane, imperturbable, always in control, invulnerable, it seemed, to everything, except the murderer's bullet. RFK was far more vulnerable. One wanted to protect him; one never felt that Jack needed protection.
>
> In Bobby's case the contrast between the myth and the man could not have been greater. He was supposed to be hard, ruthless, unfeeling, unyielding, a grudge-bearer, a hater. In fact, he was an exceptionally gentle and considerate man, the most bluntly honest man I have ever encountered in politics, a profoundly idealistic man and an extremely funny man. I loved Bobby, I cannot bear the thought that he, too, is gone.

It is fascinating to me, as an American and as a historian, how Bobby Kennedy's memory has survived these many years. I think it is the feeling he left behind. We see him as a strong leader but also as a vulnerable human being.

George Stevens Jr., a friend of Bobby's who was close by him near the end, wrote me this for this book:

> I believe Bobby's death in 1968 was consequential for America. His voice was being heard by the young and the working class and his political skill and inspiring leadership would have pulled the country together.
>
> One of the most searing moments in my life was having the television on when Frank Mankiewicz walked to a microphone outside the Good Samaritan Hospital and addressed the press with eloquent brevity. "Senator Robert Francis Kennedy died at 1:44 a.m., today June 6, 1968. He was forty-two years old."

We know we are in a more disturbing country today in 2025. We need some of Bobby's spirit and, yes, some of his rage.

Note on Sources

My resources for *Lessons from Bobby* begin with "RFK with Tears," a June 6, 1993, article I wrote for the *San Francisco Examiner*. That was twenty-five years after his assassination in Los Angeles.

Other source material I relied on includes my other books on the Kennedys: *Bobby Kennedy: A Raging Spirit*; *Kennedy & Nixon: The Rivalry that Shaped Postwar America*; and *Jack Kennedy: Elusive Hero*.

I also drew upon *Profiles in Courage* by John F. Kennedy; *"An Honorable Profession": A Tribute to Robert F. Kennedy*, edited by Pierre Salinger, Edwin Guthman, Frank Mankiewicz, and John Seigenthaler; *Robert Kennedy and His Times* by Arthur M. Schlesinger Jr.; *The Nine of Us: Growing Up Kennedy* by Jean Kennedy Smith; Jack Newfield's *RFK: A Memoir*; *Bobby*

Kennedy: The Making of a Liberal Icon by Larry Tye; and *Set Your Compass True: The Wisdom of John, Robert, and Edward Kennedy*, compiled by Signe Bergstrom. In the last chapter of the book, I relied on George Stevens Jr. He and his wife, Elizabeth, were great friends of Bobby and Ethel.

Appendix: The Speeches

Bobby Kennedy had a brief moment in the national spotlight. It began at the 1964 Democratic National Convention when he paid tribute to his brother President Kennedy. It ended when his younger brother Ted did the same for him. The words spoken in the between years include his greatest: the "ripples of hope" speech to the youth of South Africa and his campaign stop in Indianapolis, the evening of Martin Luther King Jr.'s assassination. Lines from both mark his gravesite at Arlington National Cemetery. Reading Bobby's words today gives them a powerful new urgency. They are shown here in their original style with some punctuation changed for clarity.

Tribute to John F. Kennedy at the Democratic National Convention

Robert F. Kennedy

Atlantic City, New Jersey

August 27, 1964

Mr. Chairman, I wish to speak just for a few moments.

I first want to thank all of you delegates to the Democratic National Convention and the supporters of the Democratic Party for all that you did for President John F. Kennedy.

I want to express my appreciation to you for the efforts that you made on his behalf at the convention four years ago, the efforts that you made on his behalf for his election in November of 1960, and perhaps most importantly, the encouragement and the strength that you gave him after he was elected President of the United States.

I know that it was a source of the greatest strength to him to know that there were thousands of people all over the United States who were together with him, dedicated to certain principles and to certain ideals.

No matter what talent an individual possesses, what energy he might have, no matter how much integrity and how much honesty he might have, if he is by himself, and particularly a political figure, he can accomplish very little. But if he is sustained, as President Kennedy was, by the Democratic Party all over the United States, dedicated to the same things that he was attempting to accomplish, he can accomplish a great deal.

No one knew that more than President John F. Kennedy. He used to take great pride in telling of the trip that Thomas Jefferson and James Madison made up the Hudson River in 1800 on a botanical expedition searching for butterflies; that they ended up down in New York City and that they formed the Democratic Party.

He took great pride in the fact that the Democratic Party was the oldest political Party in the world, and he knew that this linkage of Madison and Jefferson with the leaders in New York combined the North and South, and combined the industrial areas of the country with the rural farms, and that this combination was always dedicated to progress, and all of our Presidents have been dedicated to progress.

He thought of Thomas Jefferson in the Louisiana Purchase, and also when Jefferson realized that the United States could not remain on the Eastern Seaboard and sent Lewis and Clark to the West

Coast; of Andrew Jackson; of Woodrow Wilson; of Franklin Roosevelt, who saved our citizens who were in great despair because of the financial crisis; of Harry Truman, who not only spoke but acted for freedom.

So, when he became President he not only had his own principles and his own ideals but he had the strength of the Democratic Party. As President he wanted to do something for the mentally ill and the mentally retarded; for those who were not covered by Social Security; for those who were not receiving an adequate minimum wage; for those who did not have adequate housing; for our elderly people who had difficulty paying their medical bills; for our fellow citizens who are not white and who had difficulty living in this society. To all this he dedicated himself.

But he realized also that in order for us to make progress here at home, that we had to be strong overseas, that our military strength had to be strong. He said one time, "Only when our arms are sufficient, without doubt, can we be certain, without doubt, that they will never have to be employed." So when we had the crisis with the Soviet Union and the Communist Bloc in October of 1962, the Soviet Union withdrew their missiles and bombers from Cuba.

Even beyond that, his idea really was that this country, that this world, should be a better place when we turned it over to the next generation than when we inherited it from the last generation. That is why—with all of the other efforts that he made—the Test Ban Treaty, which was done with Averell Harriman, was so important to him.

And that's why he made such an effort and was committed to the young people not only of the United States but to the young people of the world. And in all of these efforts you were there, all of you.

When there were difficulties, you sustained him.

When there were periods of crisis, you stood beside him. When there were periods of happiness, you laughed with him. And when there were periods of sorrow, you comforted him. I realize that as individuals we can't just look back, that we must look forward. When I think of President Kennedy, I think of what Shakespeare said in *Romeo and Juliet*:

"When he shall die take him and cut him out into stars and he shall make the face of heaven so fine that all the world will be in love with night and pay no worship to the garish sun."

I realize that as individuals, and even more

important, as a political party and as a country, we can't just look to the past, we must look to the future.

So I join with you in realizing that what started four years ago—what everyone here started four years ago—that is to be sustained; that is to be continued.

The same effort and the same energy and the same dedication that was given to President John F. Kennedy must be given to President Lyndon Johnson and Hubert Humphrey.

If we make that evident, it will not only be for the benefit of the Democratic Party, but, far more important, it will be for the benefit of this whole country.

When we look at this film [*A Tribute to John F. Kennedy*] we must think that President Kennedy once said:

"We have the capacity to make this the best generation in the history of mankind, or make it the last."

If we do our duty, if we meet our responsibilities and our obligations, not just as Democrats, but as American citizens in our local cities and towns and farms and our states and in the country as a whole, then this generation of Americans is going to be the best generation in the history of mankind.

He often quoted from Robert Frost—and said it applied to himself—but we could apply it to the Democratic Party and to all of us as individuals:

"The woods are lovely, dark and deep, / But I have promises to keep, / And miles to go before I sleep, / And miles to go before I sleep."

Mrs. Kennedy has asked that this film be dedicated to all of you and to all the others throughout the country who helped make John F. Kennedy President of the United States.

I thank you.

Day of Affirmation Address

Robert F. Kennedy

University of Cape Town

Cape Town, South Africa

June 6, 1966

Mr. Chancellor, Mr. Vice Chancellor, Professor Robertson, Mr. Diamond, Mr. Daniel, Ladies and Gentlemen:

I come here this evening because of my deep interest and affection for a land settled by the Dutch in the mid-seventeenth century, then taken over by the British, and at last independent; a land in which the native inhabitants were at first subdued, but relations with whom remain a problem to this day; a land which defined itself on a hostile frontier; a land which has tamed rich natural resources through the energetic application of modern technology; a land which was once the importer of slaves, and now must struggle to wipe out the last traces of that former bondage. I refer, of course, to the United States of America.

But I am glad to come here, and my wife and I and all of our party are glad to come here to South

Africa, and we are glad to come here to Cape Town. I am already greatly enjoying my stay and my visit here. I am making an effort to meet and exchange views with people of all walks of life, and all segments of South African opinion—including those who represent the views of the government. Today I am glad to meet with the National Union of South African Students. For a decade, NUSAS has stood and worked for the principles of the Universal Declaration of Human Rights—principles which embody the collective hopes of men of good will all around the globe.

Your work, at home and in international student affairs, has brought great credit to yourselves and to your country. I know the National Student Association in the United States feels a particularly close relationship with this organization. And I wish to thank especially Mr. Ian Robertson [NUSAS president], who first extended this invitation on behalf of NUSAS. I wish to thank him for his kindness to me in inviting me. I am very sorry that he cannot be with us here this evening. I was happy to have had the opportunity to meet and speak with him earlier this evening, and I presented him with a copy of *Profiles in Courage*, which was a book that was written by

President John Kennedy and was signed to him by President Kennedy's widow, Mrs. John Kennedy.

This is a Day of Affirmation—a celebration of liberty. We stand here in the name of freedom.

At the heart of that Western freedom and democracy is the belief that the individual man, the child of God, is the touchstone of value, and all society, all groups and states, exist for that person's benefit. Therefore the enlargement of liberty for individual human beings must be the supreme goal and the abiding practice of any Western society.

The first element of this individual liberty is the freedom of speech; the right to express and communicate ideas, to set oneself apart from the dumb beasts of field and forest; the right to recall governments to their duties and to their obligations; above all, the right to affirm one's membership and allegiance to the body politic—to society—to the men with whom we share our land, our heritage and our children's future.

Hand in hand with freedom of speech goes the power to be heard—to share in the decisions of government which shape men's lives. Everything that makes man's life worthwhile—family, work, education, a place to rear one's children and a place to rest one's head—all this depends on the decisions of government; all can be swept away by a government which does not heed the demands of its people, and I mean all of its people. Therefore, the essential humanity of man can be protected and preserved only where government must answer—not just to the wealthy, not just to those of a particular religion, not just to those of a particular race, but to all of the people.

And even government by the consent of the governed, as in our own Constitution, must be limited in its power to act against its people: so that there may be no interference with the right to worship, but also no interference with the security of the home; no arbitrary imposition of pains or penalties on an ordinary citizen by officials high or low; no restriction on the freedom of men to seek education or to seek work or opportunity of any kind, so that each man may become all that he is capable of becoming.

These are the sacred rights of Western society. These were the essential differences between us and Nazi Germany as they were between Athens and Persia.

They are the essence of our differences with communism today. I am unalterably opposed to communism because it exalts the state over the individual and over the family, and because its system contains a lack of freedom of speech, of protest, of religion, and of the press, which is characteristic of a totalitarian regime. The way of opposition to communism, however, is not to imitate its dictatorship, but to enlarge individual human freedom. There are those in every land who would label as "communist" every threat to their privilege. But may I say to you, as I have seen on my travels in all sections of the world, reform is not communism. And the denial of freedom, in whatever name, only strengthens the very communism it claims to oppose.

Many nations have set forth their own definitions and declarations of these principles. And there have often been wide and tragic gaps between promise and performance, ideal and reality. Yet the great ideals have constantly recalled us to our own duties. And—with painful slowness—we in the United States have extended and enlarged the meaning and the practice of freedom to all of our people.

For two centuries, my own country has struggled to overcome the self-imposed handicap of prejudice and discrimination based on nationality, on social class or race—discrimination profoundly repugnant to the theory and to the command of our Constitution. Even as my father grew up in Boston, Massachusetts, signs told him "No Irish Need Apply." Two generations later, President Kennedy became the first Irish Catholic, and the first Catholic, to head the nation; but how many men of ability had, before 1961, been denied the opportunity to contribute to the nation's progress because they were Catholic, or because they were of Irish extraction? How many sons of Italian or Jewish or Polish parents slumbered in the slums—untaught, unlearned, their potential lost forever to our nation and to the human race? Even today, what price will we pay before we have assured full opportunity to millions of Negro Americans?

In the last five years we have done more to assure equality to our Negro citizens and to help the deprived, both white and black, than in the hundred years before that time. But much, much more remains to be done.

For there are millions of Negroes untrained for the simplest of jobs, and thousands every day denied their full and equal rights under the law; and the violence of the disinherited, the insulted, the injured, looms over the streets of Harlem and of Watts and of the South Side of Chicago.

But a Negro American trains as an astronaut, one of mankind's first explorers into outer space; another is the chief barrister of the United States government, and dozens sit on the benches of our court; and another, Dr. Martin Luther King, is the second man of African descent to win the Nobel Peace Prize for his non-violent efforts for social justice between all of the races.

We have passed laws prohibiting discrimination in education, in employment, in housing; but these laws alone cannot overcome the heritage of centuries—of broken families and stunted children, and poverty and degradation and pain.

So the road toward equality of freedom is not easy, and great cost and danger march alongside all of us. We are committed to peaceful and non-violent change and that is important for all to understand—though change is unsettling. Still, even in the turbulence of protest and struggle is greater hope for the future, as men learn to claim and achieve for themselves the rights formerly petitioned from others.

And most important of all, all the panoply of government power has been committed to the goal of equality before the law—as we are now committing ourselves to the achievement of equal opportunity in fact.

We must recognize the full human equality of all of our people—before God, before the law, and in the councils of government. We must do this, not because it is economically advantageous—although it is; not because the laws of God command it—although they do; not because people in other lands wish it so. We must do it for the single and fundamental reason that it is the right thing to do.

We recognize that there are problems and obstacles before the fulfillment of these ideals in the United States as we recognize that other nations, in Latin America and in Asia and in Africa, have their own political, economic, and social problems, their unique barriers to the elimination of injustices.

In some, there is concern that change will submerge the rights of a minority, particularly where that minority is of a different race than that of the majority. We in the United States believe in the protection of minorities; we recognize the contributions that they can make and the leadership that they can provide; and we do not believe that any people—whether majority or minority, or individual human beings—are "expendable" in the cause of theory or of policy. We recognize also that justice between men and nations is imperfect, and that humanity sometimes progresses very slowly indeed.

All do not develop in the same manner and at the same pace. Nations, like men, often march to the beat of different drummers, and the precise solutions of the

United States can neither be dictated nor transplanted to others, and that is not our intention. What is important, however, is that all nations must march toward increasing freedom; toward justice for all; toward a society strong and flexible enough to meet the demands of all of its people, whatever their race, and the demands of a world of immense and dizzying change that face us all.

In a few hours, the plane that brought me to this country crossed over oceans and countries which have been a crucible of human history. In minutes we traced migrations of men over thousands of years; seconds, the briefest glimpse, and we passed battlefields on which millions of men once struggled and died. We could see no national boundaries, no vast gulfs or high walls dividing people from people; only nature and the works of man—homes and factories and farms—everywhere reflecting man's common effort to enrich his life. Everywhere new technology and communications bring men and nations closer together, the concerns of one inevitably become the concerns of all. And our new closeness is stripping away the false masks, the illusion of differences, which is the root of injustice and of hate and of war. Only earthbound man still clings to the dark and poisoning superstition that his world is bounded by the nearest hill, his universe ends at river's shore, his common humanity is enclosed in the tight circle of those who share his town or his views and the color of his skin.

It is your job, the task of young people in this world, to strip the last remnants of that ancient, cruel belief from the civilization of man.

Each nation has different obstacles and different goals, shaped by the vagaries of history and of experience. Yet as I talk to young people around the world, I am impressed not by the diversity but by the closeness of their goals, their desires, and their concerns and their hope for the future. There is discrimination in New York, the racial inequality of apartheid in South Africa, and serfdom in the mountains of Peru. People starve to death in the streets of India; a former Prime Minister is summarily executed in the Congo; intellectuals go to jail in Russia; and thousands are slaughtered in Indonesia; wealth is lavished on armaments everywhere in the world. These are different evils, but they are the common works of man. They reflect the imperfections of human justice, the inadequacy of human compassion, the defectiveness of our sensibility toward the sufferings of our fellows; they mark the limit of our ability to use knowledge for the well-being of our fellow human beings throughout the world. And therefore they call upon common qualities of conscience and indignation, a shared determination to wipe away the unnecessary sufferings of our fellow human beings at home and around the world.

It is these qualities which make of our youth today the only true international community. More than this I think that we could agree on what kind of a world we would all want to build. It would be a world of independent nations, moving toward international community, each of which protected and respected the basic human freedoms. It would be a world which demanded of each government that it accept its responsibility to ensure social justice. It would be a world of constantly accelerating economic progress—not material welfare as an end in and of itself, but as a means to liberate the capacity of every human being to pursue his talents and to pursue his hopes. It would, in short, be a world that we would all be proud to have built.

Just to the north of here are lands of challenge and of opportunity—rich in natural resources, land and minerals and people. Yet they are also lands confronted by the greatest odds—overwhelming ignorance, internal tensions and strife, and great obstacles of climate and geography. Many of these nations, as colonies, were oppressed and were exploited. Yet they have not estranged themselves from the broad traditions of the West; they are hoping and they are gambling their progress and their stability on the chance that we will meet our responsibilities to them, to help them overcome their poverty.

In the world we would like to build, South Africa could play an outstanding role, and a role of leadership in that effort. This country is without question a preeminent repository of the wealth and the knowledge and the skill of this continent. Here are the greater part of Africa's research scientists and steel production, most of its reservoirs of coal and of electric power. Many South Africans have made major contributions to African technical development and world science; the names of some are known wherever men seek to eliminate the ravages of tropical disease and of pestilence. In your faculties and councils, here in this very audience, are hundreds and thousands of men and women who could transform the lives of millions for all time to come.

But the help and the leadership of South Africa or of the United States cannot be accepted if we—within our own countries or in our relationships with others—deny individual integrity, human dignity, and the common humanity of man. If we would lead outside our own borders; if we would help those who need our assistance; if we would meet our responsibilities to mankind; we must first, all of us, demolish the borders which history has erected between men within our own nations—barriers of race and religion, social class and ignorance.

Our answer is the world's hope; it is to rely on youth. The cruelties and the obstacles of this swiftly changing planet will not yield to obsolete dogmas and outworn slogans. It cannot be moved by those who cling to a present which is already dying, who prefer the illusion of security to the excitement and danger which comes with even the most peaceful progress. This world demands the qualities of youth: not a time of life but a state of mind, a temper of the will, a quality of the imagination, a predominance of courage over timidity, of the appetite for adventure over the life of ease—a man like the Chancellor of this University. It is a revolutionary world that we all live in; and thus, as I have said in Latin America and in Asia and in Europe and in my own country, the United States, it is the young people who must take the lead. Thus you, and your young compatriots everywhere have had thrust upon you a greater burden of responsibility than any generation that has ever lived.

"There is," said an Italian philosopher, "nothing more difficult to take in hand, more perilous to conduct, or more uncertain in its success than to take the lead in the introduction of a new order of things." Yet this is the measure of the task of your generation and the road is strewn with many dangers.

First is the danger of futility; the belief there is nothing one man or one woman can do against the enormous array of the world's ills—against misery, against ignorance, or injustice and violence. Yet many of the world's great movements, of thought and action, have flowed from the work of a single man. A young monk began the Protestant reformation, a young general extended an empire from Macedonia to the borders of the earth, and a young woman reclaimed the territory of France. It was a young Italian explorer who discovered the New World, and 32-year-old Thomas Jefferson who proclaimed that all men are created equal. "Give me a place to stand," said Archimedes, "and I will move the world." These men moved the world, and so can we all. Few will have the greatness to bend history; but each of us can work to change a small portion of the events, and in the total of all these acts will be written the history of this generation. Thousands of Peace Corps volunteers are making a difference in the isolated villages and the city slums of dozens of countries. Thousands of unknown men and women in Europe resisted the occupation of the Nazis and many died, but all added to the ultimate strength and freedom of their countries. It is from numberless diverse acts of courage such as these that human history is thus shaped. Each time a man stands up for an ideal, or acts to improve the lot of others, or strikes out against injustice, he sends forth a tiny ripple of hope, and crossing each other from a million different centers of energy and daring, those ripples build a current which can sweep down the mightiest walls of oppression and resistance.

"If Athens shall appear great to you," said Pericles, "consider then that her glories were purchased by valiant men, and by men who learned their duty." That is the source of all greatness in all societies, and it is the key to progress in our time.

The second danger is that of expediency; of those who say that hopes and beliefs must bend before immediate necessities. Of course if we must act effectively we must deal with the world as it is. We must get things done. But if there was one thing that President Kennedy stood for that touched the most profound feeling of young people around the world, it was the belief that idealism, high aspiration and deep convictions are not incompatible with the most practical and efficient of programs—that there is no basic inconsistency between ideals and realistic possibilities—no separation between the deepest desires of heart and of mind and the rational application of human effort to human problems. It is not realistic or hard-headed to solve problems and take action unguided by ultimate moral aims and values, although we all know some who claim that it is so. In my judgment, it is thoughtless folly. For it ignores the realities of human faith and of passion and of belief; forces ultimately more powerful than all the calculations of our economists or of our generals. Of course to adhere to standards, to idealism, to vision in the face of immediate dangers, takes great courage and takes self-confidence. But we also know that only those who dare to fail greatly, can ever achieve greatly.

It is this new idealism which is also, I believe, the common heritage of a generation which has learned that while efficiency can lead to the camps at Auschwitz, or the streets of Budapest, only the ideals of humanity and love can climb the hills of the Acropolis.

And a third danger is timidity. Few men are willing to brave the disapproval of their fellows, the censure of their colleagues, the wrath of their society. Moral courage is a rarer commodity than bravery in battle or great intelligence. Yet it is the one essential, vital quality for those who seek to change the world which yields most painfully to change. Aristotle tells us, "At the Olympic games it is not the finest or the strongest men who are crowned, but those who enter the lists . . . so too in the life of the honorable and the good it is they who act rightly who win the prize." I believe that in this generation those with the courage to enter the conflict will find themselves with companions in every corner of the world.

For the fortunate amongst us, the fourth danger, my friends, is comfort; the temptation to follow the easy and familiar path of personal ambition and financial success so grandly spread before those who have the privilege of an education. But that is not the road history has marked out for us. There is a Chinese curse which says "May he live in interesting times." Like it or not, we live in interesting times. They are times of danger and uncertainty; but they are also the most creative of any time in the history of mankind. And everyone here will ultimately be judged—will ultimately judge himself—on the effort he has contributed to building a new world society and the extent to which his ideals and goals have shaped that effort.

So we part, I to my country and you to remain. We are—if a man of forty can claim the privilege—fellow members of the world's largest younger generation. Each of us have our own work to do. I know at times you must feel very alone with your problems and with your difficulties. But I want to say how impressed I am with what you stand for and for the effort that you are making; and I say this not just for myself, but men and women all over the world. And I hope you will often take heart from the knowledge that you are joined with your fellow young people in every land, they struggling with their problems and you with yours, but all joined in a common purpose; that, like the young people of my own country and of every country that I have visited, you are all in many ways more closely united to the brothers of your time than to the older generation in any of these nations; you are determined to build a better future. President Kennedy was speaking to the young people of America, but beyond them, to young people everywhere, when he said, "The energy, the faith, the devotion which we bring to this endeavor will light our country and all who serve it—and the glow from that fire can truly light the world."

And, he added, "With a good conscience our only sure reward, with history the final judge of our deeds, let us go forth to lead the land we love, asking His blessing and His help, but knowing that here on earth God's work must truly be our own."

I thank you.

Announcement of Candidacy for President

Robert F. Kennedy

Washington, DC

March 16, 1968

I am announcing today my candidacy for the presidency of the United States.

I do not run for the presidency merely to oppose any man but to propose new policies. I run because I am convinced that this country is on a perilous course and because I have such strong feelings about what must be done, and I feel that I'm obliged to do all that I can.

I run to seek new policies—policies to end the bloodshed in Vietnam and in our cities, policies to close the gaps that now exist between black and white, between rich and poor, between young and old, in this country and around the rest of the world.

I run for the presidency because I want the Democratic Party and the United States of America to stand for hope instead of despair, for reconciliation of men instead of the growing risk of world war.

I run because it is now unmistakably clear that we can change these disastrous, divisive policies only by changing the men who are now making them. For the reality of recent events in Vietnam has been glossed over with illusions.

The report of the Riot Commission has been largely ignored.

The crisis in gold, the crisis in our cities, the crisis in our farms and in our ghettos have all been met with too little and too late.

No one who knows what I know about the extraordinary demands of the presidency can be certain that any mortal can adequately fill that position.

But my service on the National Security Council during the Cuban Missile Crisis, the Berlin crisis of 1961 and 1962 and later, the negotiations on Laos and on the Nuclear Test Ban, have taught me something about both the uses and the limitations of military power, about the value of negotiations with allies and with enemies, about the opportunities and the dangers which await our nation in many corners of the globe in which I have traveled.

As a member of the cabinet and a member of the Senate, I have seen the inexcusable and ugly deprivation which causes children to starve in Mississippi; black citizens to riot in Watts; young Indians to commit suicide on their reservations because they've lacked all hope and they feel they have no future; and proud and able-bodied families to wait out their lives in empty idleness in eastern Kentucky.

I have traveled and I have listened to the young people of our nation and felt their anger about the war that they are sent to fight and about the world that they are about to inherit.

In private talks and in public, I have tried in vain to alter our course in Vietnam before it further saps our spirit and our manpower, further raises the risks of wider war, and further destroys the country and the people it was meant to save.

I cannot stand aside from the contest that will decide our nation's future and our children's future.

The remarkable New Hampshire campaign of Senator Eugene McCarthy has proven how deep are the present divisions within our party and within our country. Until that was publicly clear, my presence in the race would have been seen as a clash of personalities rather than issues.

But now that that fight is won and over policies which I have long been challenging, I must enter that race. The fight is just beginning, and I believe that I can win. . . .

Finally, my decision reflects no personal animosity

or disrespect toward President Johnson. He served President Kennedy with the utmost loyalty and was extremely kind to me and members of my family in the difficult months which followed the events of November of 1963.

I have often commended his efforts in health, in education, and in many other areas, and I have the deepest sympathy for the burden that he carries today.

But the issue is not personal. It is our profound differences over where we are heading and what we want to accomplish.

I do not lightly dismiss the dangers and the difficulties of challenging an incumbent president. But these are not ordinary times and this is not an ordinary election.

At stake is not simply the leadership of our party and even our country. It is our right to the moral leadership of this planet.

Remarks at the University of Kansas

Robert F. Kennedy

Lawrence, Kansas

March 18, 1968

Thank you very much. Chancellor, Governor and Mrs. Docking, Senator and Mrs. Pearson, ladies and gentlemen and my friends, I'm very pleased to be here. I'm really not here to make a speech. I've come because I came from Kansas State and they want to send their love to all of you. They did. That's all they talk about over there, how much they love you. Actually, I want to establish the fact that I am not an alumnus of Villanova.

I'm very pleased and very touched, as my wife is, at your warm reception here. I think of my colleagues in the United States Senate, I think of my friends there, and I think of the warmth that exists in the Senate of the United States—I don't know why you're laughing—I was sick last year and I received a message from the Senate of the United States which said: "We hope you recover," and the vote was forty-two to forty.

And then they took a poll in one of the financial magazines of five hundred of the largest businessmen in the United States, to ask them what political leader they most admired, who they wanted to see as President of the United States, and I received one vote, and I understand they're looking for him. I could take all my supporters to lunch, but I'm—I don't know whether you're going to like what I'm going to say today but I just want you to remember, as you look back upon this day, and when it comes to a question of who you're going to support—that it was a Kennedy who got you out of class.

I am very pleased to be here with my colleagues. Senator Pearson, who I think has contributed so much in the Senate of the United States—who has fought for the interests of Kansas and has had a distinguished career, and I'm very proud to be associated with him. And Senator Carlson, who is not here, who is one of the most respected members of the Senate of the United States—respected not just on the Republican side—by the Democratic side, by all of his colleagues, and I'm pleased and proud to be in the Senate with Senator Carlson of the State of Kansas.

And I'm happy to be here with an old friend, Governor Docking. I don't think there was anyone that was more committed to President Kennedy and made more of an effort under the most adverse circumstances and with the most difficult of situations than his father, who was then Governor of the State of Kansas—nobody I worked with more closely, myself, when I was in Los Angeles. We weren't 100 percent successful, but that was a relationship that I will always value, and I know how highly President Kennedy valued it and I'm very pleased to see him—and to have seen his mother, Mrs. Docking, today also, so I'm very pleased to be in his State.

And then I'm pleased to be here because I like to see all of you, in addition.

In 1824, when Thomas Hart Benton was urging in Congress the development of Iowa and other Western territories, he was opposed by Daniel Webster, the Senator from Massachusetts. "What," asked Webster, "what do we want with this vast and worthless area? This region of savages and wild beasts. Of deserts of shifting sands and of whirlwinds. Of dust, and of cactus and of prairie dogs.

"To what use," he said, "could we ever hope to put these great deserts? I will never vote for one cent from the public treasury, to place the West one inch closer to Boston than it is now." And that is why I am here today, instead of my brother Edward.

I'm glad to come here to the home of the man who publicly wrote: "If our colleges and universities do not breed men who riot, who rebel, who attack life with all the youthful vision and vigor, then there is something wrong with our colleges. The more riots that come out of our college campuses, the better the world for tomorrow." And despite all the accusations against me, those words were not written by me, they were written by that notorious seditionist, William Allen White. And I know what great affection this university has for him. He is an honored man today, here on your campus and around the rest of the nation. But when he lived and wrote, he was reviled as an extremist and worse. For he spoke, he spoke as he believed. He did not conceal his concern in comforting words. He did not delude his readers or himself with false hopes and with illusions. This spirit of honest confrontation is what America needs today. It has been missing all too often in the recent years and it is one of the reasons that I run for President of the United States.

For we as a people, we as a people, are strong enough, we are brave enough to be told the truth of where we stand. And this country needs honesty and candor in its political life and from the President of the United States. But I don't want to run for the presidency—I don't want America to make the critical choice of direction and leadership this year without confronting that truth. I don't want to win support of votes by hiding the American condition in false hopes or illusions. I want us to find out the promise of the future, what we can accomplish here in the United States, what this country does stand for and what is expected of us in the years ahead. And I also want us to know and examine where we've gone wrong. And I want all of us, young and old, to have a chance to build a better country and change the direction of the United States of America.

This morning I spoke about the war in Vietnam, and I will speak briefly about it in a few moments. But there is much more to this critical election year than the war in Vietnam.

It is, at a root, the root of all of it, the national soul of the United States. The President calls it "restlessness." Our cabinet officers such as John Gardner and others tell us that America is deep in a malaise of spirit: discouraging initiative, paralyzing will and action, and dividing Americans from one another, by their age, their views and by the color of their skin, and I don't think we have to accept that here in the United States of America.

Demonstrators shout down government officials and the government answers by drafting demonstrators. Anarchists threaten to burn the country down and some have begun to try, while tanks have patrolled American streets and machine guns have fired at American children. I don't think this is a satisfying situation for the United States of America.

Our young people, the best educated and the best comforted in our history, turn from the Peace Corps and public commitment of a few years ago to lives of disengagement and despair, many of them turned on with drugs and turned off on America—none of them here, of course, at Kansas. Right?

All around us, all around us—not just on the question of Vietnam, not just on the question of the cities, not just on the question of poverty, not just on the problems of race relations—but all around us, and why you are so concerned and why you are so disturbed—the fact is, that men have lost confidence in themselves, in each other, it is confidence which has sustained us so much in the past—rather than answer the cries of deprivation and despair—cries which the President's Commission on Civil Disorders tells us could split our nation finally asunder—rather than answer these desperate cries, hundreds of communities and millions of citizens are looking for their answers, to force and repression and private gunstocks—so that we confront our fellow citizen across impassable barriers of hostility and mistrust and again, I don't believe that we have to accept that. I don't believe that it's necessary in the United States of America. I think that we can work together—I don't think that we have to shoot at each other, to beat each other, to curse each other and criticize each other; I think that we can do better in this country. And that is why I run for President of the United States.

And if we seem powerless to stop this growing division between Americans, who at least confront one another, there are millions more living in the hidden places, whose names and faces are completely unknown—but I have seen these other Americans—I have seen children in Mississippi starving, their bodies so crippled from hunger and their minds have been so destroyed for their whole life, that they will have no future. I have seen children in Mississippi—here in the United States—with a gross national product of 800 billion dollars—I have seen children in the Delta area of Mississippi with distended stomachs, whose faces are covered with sores from starvation, and we haven't developed a policy so we can get enough food so that they can live, so that their children, so that their lives, are not destroyed. I don't think that's acceptable in the United States of America, and I think we need a change.

I have seen Indians living on their bare and meager reservations, with no jobs, with an unemployment rate of 80 percent, and with so little hope for the future, so little hope for the future that for young people, for young men and women in their teens, the greatest cause of death amongst them is suicide.

That they end their lives by killing themselves—I don't think that we have to accept that—for the first Americans, for this minority here in the United States. If young boys and girls are so filled with despair when they're going to high school and feel that their lives are so hopeless and that nobody's going to care for them, nobody's going to be involved with them, and nobody's going to bother with them, that they either hang themselves, shoot themselves, or kill themselves—I don't think that's acceptable and I think the United States of America, I think the American people, I think we can do much, much better. And I run for the presidency because of that. I run for the presidency because I have seen proud men in the hills of Appalachia who wish only to work in dignity, but they cannot, for the mines are closed and their jobs are gone and no one—neither industry, nor labor, nor government—has cared enough to help.

I think we here in this country, with the unselfish spirit that exists in the United States of America, I think we can do better here also.

I have seen the people of the black ghetto, listening to ever greater promises of equality and of justice, as they sit in the same decaying schools and huddled in the same filthy rooms—without heat—warding off the cold and warding off the rats.

If we believe that we, as Americans, are bound together by a common concern for each other, then an urgent national priority is upon us. We must begin to end the disgrace of this other America.

And this is one of the great tasks of leadership for us, as individuals and citizens this year. But even if we act to erase material poverty, there is another greater task: it is to confront the poverty of satisfaction—purpose and dignity—that afflicts us all. Too much and for too long, we seemed to have surrendered personal excellence and community values in the mere accumulation of material things. Our gross national product now is over eight hundred billion dollars a year, but that gross national product—if we judge the United States of America by that—that gross national product counts air pollution and cigarette advertising, and ambulances to clear our highways of carnage. It counts special locks for our doors and the jails for the people who break them. It counts the destruction of the redwood and the loss of our natural wonder in chaotic sprawl. It counts napalm and it counts nuclear warheads and armored cars for the police to fight the riots in our cities. It counts Whitman's rifle and Speck's knife, and the television programs which glorify violence in order to sell toys to our children. Yet the gross national product does not allow for the health of our children, the quality of their education or the joy of their play. It does not include the beauty of our poetry or the strength of our marriages, the intelligence of our public debate or the integrity of our public officials. It measures neither our wit nor our courage, neither our wisdom nor our learning, neither our compassion nor our devotion to our country. It measures everything, in short, except that which makes life worthwhile. And it can tell us everything about America except why we are proud that we are Americans.

If this is true here at home, so it is true elsewhere in the world. From the beginning our proudest boast has been the promise of Jefferson, that we here in this country would be the best hope of mankind. And now, as we look at the war in Vietnam, we wonder if we still hold a decent respect for the opinions of mankind and whether the opinion maintained a decent respect for us, or whether, like Athens of old, we will forfeit sympathy and support, and ultimately our very security, in the single-minded pursuit of our own goals and our own objectives. I do not want, and I do believe that most Americans do not want, to sell out America's interest to simply withdraw—to raise the white flag of surrender in Vietnam. That would be unacceptable to us as a people, and unacceptable to us as a country. But I am concerned about the course of action that we are presently following in South Vietnam. I am concerned, I am concerned about the fact that this has been made America's War. It was said, a number of years ago, that this is "their war," "this is the war of the South Vietnamese," that "we can help them, but we can't win it for them," but over the period of the last three years we have made the war and the struggle in South Vietnam our war, and I think that's unacceptable.

I don't accept the idea that this is just a military action, that this is just a military effort, and every time we have had difficulties in South Vietnam and Southeast Asia we have had only one response, we have had only one way to deal with it—month after month—year after year we have dealt with it in only one way and that's to send more military men and increase our military power and I don't think that's the kind of a struggle that it is in Southeast Asia.

I think that this is a question of the people of South Vietnam, I think it's a question of the people of South Vietnam feeling it's worth their efforts—that they're going to make the sacrifice—that they feel that their country and their government is worth fighting for, and I think the developments of the last several years have shown, have demonstrated that the people of South Vietnam feel no association and no affiliation for the government of Saigon. And I don't think it's up to us here in the United States, I don't think it's up to us here in the United States to say that we're going to destroy all of South Vietnam because we have a commitment there. The commander of the American forces at Ben Tre said we had to destroy that city in order to save it. So 38,000 people were wiped out or made refugees. We here in the United States—not just the United States government, not just the commanders of and forces in South Vietnam, the United States government and every human being that's in this room—we are part of that decision and I don't think that we need do that any longer, and I think we should change our policy.

I don't want to be part of a government, I don't want to be part of the United States, I don't want to be part of the American people, and have them write of us as they wrote of Rome: "They made a desert and they called it peace."

I think that we should go to the negotiating table, and I think we should take the steps to go to the negotiating table.

And I've said it over the period of the last two years, I think that we have a chance to have negotiations, and the possibility of meaningful negotiations, but last February, a year ago, when the greatest opportunity existed for negotiations, the Administration and the President of the United States felt that the military victory was right around the corner and we sent a message to Ho Chi Minh, on February 8th of 1967, virtually asking for their unconditional surrender; we are not going to obtain the unconditional surrender of the North Vietnamese and the Viet Cong any more than they're going to obtain the unconditional surrender of the United States of America. We're going to have to negotiate, we're going to have to make compromises, we're going to have to negotiate with the National Liberation Front. But people can argue, "That's unfortunate that we have to negotiate with the

National Liberation Front," but that is a fact of life. We have three choices: We can either pull out of South Vietnam unilaterally and raise the white flag—I think that's unacceptable.

Second, we can continue to escalate, we can continue to send more men there, until we have millions and millions of more men and we can continue to bomb North Vietnam, and in my judgment we will be no nearer success, we will be no nearer victory than we are now in February of 1968.

And the third step that we can take is to go to the negotiating table. We can go to the negotiating table and not achieve everything that we wish. One of the things that we're going to have to accept as American people—but the other, the other alternative is so unacceptable—one of the things that we're going to have to accept as American people and that the United States government must accept, is that the National Liberation Front is going to play a role in the future political process of South Vietnam.

And we're going to have to negotiate with them. That they are going to play some role in the future political process of South Vietnam, that there are going to be elections, and the people of South

Vietnam are ultimately going to determine and decide their own future.

That is the course of action, that is the course of action that I would like to see. I would like to see the United States government to make it clear to the government of Saigon that we are not going to tolerate the corruption and the dishonesty. I think that we should make it clear to the government of Saigon that if we're going to draft young men, 18 years of age here in the United States, if we're going to draft young men who are 19 years old here in the United States, and we're going to send them to fight and die in Khe Sanh, that we want the government of South Vietnam to draft their 18-year-olds and their 19-year-olds.

And I want to make it clear that if the government of Saigon feels Khe Sanh or Que Son and the area in the demilitarized zone are so important, if Khe Sanh is so important to the government of Saigon, I want to see those American marines out of there and South Vietnamese troops in there.

I want to have an explanation as to why American boys killed two weeks ago in South Vietnam were three times as many—more than three times as many as the soldiers of South Vietnam. I want to understand why the casualties and the deaths over the period of the last two weeks at the height of the fighting should be so heavily American casualties, as compared to the South Vietnamese. This is their war. I think we have to make the effort to help them, I think that we have to make the effort to fight, but I don't think that we should have to carry the whole burden of that war; I think the South Vietnamese should.

And if I am elected President of the United States, with help, with your help, these are the kinds of policies that I'm going to put into operation.

We can do better here in the United States; we can do better. We can do better in our relationships to other countries around the rest of the globe. President Kennedy, when he campaigned in 1960, he talked about the loss of prestige that the United States had suffered around the rest of the globe, but look at what our condition is at the present time. The President of the United States goes to a meeting of the OAS [Organization of American States] at Montevideo—can he go into the city of Montevideo? Or can he travel through the cities of Latin America where there was such deep love and deep respect? He has to stay in a military base at Montevideo, with American ships out at sea and

American helicopters overhead in order to ensure that he's protected. I don't think that that's acceptable.

I think that we should have conditions here in the United States, and support enough for our policies, so that the President of the United States can travel freely and clearly across all the cities of this country, and not just to military bases.

I think there's more that we can do internally here. I think there's more that we can do in South Vietnam. I don't think we have to accept the situation as we have it at the moment. I think that we can do better, and I think the American people think that we can do better.

George Bernard Shaw once wrote, "Some people see things as they are and say 'Why?' I dream things that never were and say 'Why not?'"

So I come here to Kansas to ask for your help. In the difficult five months ahead before the convention in Chicago, I ask for your help and for your assistance. If you believe that the United States can do better, if you believe that we should change our course of action, if you believe that the United States stands for something here internally as well as elsewhere around the globe, I ask for your help and your assistance and your hand over the period of the next five months.

And when we win in November, and when we win in November, and we begin a new period of time for the United States of America, I want the next generation of Americans to look back upon this period and say, as they said of Plato: "Joy was in those days, but to live." Thank you very much.

Statement on Assassination of Martin Luther King Jr.

Senator Robert F. Kennedy

Indianapolis, Indiana

April 4, 1968

I have some very sad news for all of you. And that is that Martin Luther King was shot and was killed tonight in Memphis, Tennessee. Martin Luther King dedicated his life to love and to justice between fellow human beings. He died in the cause of that effort.

In this difficult day, in this difficult time for the United States, it's perhaps well to ask what kind of a nation we are, and what direction we want to move in.

For those of you who are black—considering the evidence evidently that there were white people who were responsible—you can be filled with bitterness, and with hatred, and a desire for revenge. We can move in that direction as a country, in greater polarization—black people amongst black, white people amongst white, filled with hatred toward one another.

Or we can make an effort, as Martin Luther King did, to understand and to comprehend, and to replace that violence, that stain of bloodshed that has spread across our land, with an effort to understand, compassion, and love.

For those of you who are black and are tempted to be filled with hatred and distrust at the injustice of such an act, against all white people, I would only say that I can also feel in my own heart the same kind of feeling. I had a member of my family killed—but he was killed by a white man. But we have to make an effort in the United States. We have to make an effort to understand, to get beyond or go beyond these rather difficult times.

My favorite poet was Aeschylus. He once wrote: "Even in our sleep, pain which cannot forget falls drop by drop upon the heart until, in our own despair, against our will, comes wisdom through the awful grace of God."

What we need in the United States is not division. What we need in the United States is not hatred. What we need in the United States is not violence and lawlessness, but is love and wisdom, and compassion toward one another, a feeling of justice toward those who still suffer within our country—whether they be white or whether they be black.

So I shall ask you tonight to return home, to say a prayer for the family of Martin Luther King, that's true, but more importantly to say a prayer for our own country, which all of us love—a prayer for understanding and that compassion of which I spoke.

We can do well in this country. We will have difficult times. We've had difficult times in the past. We will have difficult times in the future. It is not the end of violence. It is not the end of lawlessness, and it is not the end of disorder.

But the vast majority of white people and the vast majority of black people in this country want to live together, want to improve the quality of our life, and want justice for all human beings that abide in our land.

Let us dedicate ourselves to what the Greeks wrote so many years ago: to tame the savageness of man and make gentle the life of this world.

Let us dedicate ourselves to that, and say a prayer for our country and for our people. Thank you very much.

Remarks to the Cleveland City Club
Robert F. Kennedy
Cleveland, Ohio
April 5, 1968

This is a time of shame and sorrow. It is not a day for politics. I have saved this one opportunity to speak briefly to you about this mindless menace of violence in America which again stains our land and every one of our lives.

It is not the concern of any one race. The victims of the violence are black and white, rich and poor, young and old, famous and unknown. They are, most important of all, human beings whom other human beings loved and needed. No one—no matter where he lives or what he does—can be certain who will suffer from some senseless act of bloodshed. And yet it goes on and on.

Why? What has violence ever accomplished? What has it ever created? No martyr's cause has ever been stilled by his assassin's bullet.

No wrongs have ever been righted by riots and civil disorders. A sniper is only a coward, not a hero; and an uncontrolled, uncontrollable mob is only the voice of madness, not the voice of the people.

Whenever any American's life is taken by another American unnecessarily—whether it is done in the name of the law or in the defiance of the law, by one man or a gang, in cold blood or in passion, in an attack of violence or in response to violence—whenever we tear at the fabric of life which another man has painfully and clumsily woven for himself and his children, the whole nation is degraded.

"Among free men," said Abraham Lincoln, "there can be no successful appeal from the ballot to the bullet; and those who take such appeal are sure to lose their cause and pay the costs."

Yet we seemingly tolerate a rising level of violence that ignores our common humanity and our claims to civilization alike. We calmly accept newspaper reports of civilian slaughter in far off lands. We glorify killing on movie and television screens and call it entertainment. We make it easy for men of all shades of sanity to acquire weapons and ammunition they desire.

Too often we honor swagger and bluster and the wielders of force; too often we excuse those who are willing to build their own lives on the shattered dreams of others. Some Americans who preach nonviolence abroad fail to practice it here at home.

Some who accuse others of inciting riots have by their own conduct invited them.

Some look for scapegoats, others look for conspiracies, but this much is clear; violence breeds violence, repression brings retaliation, and only a cleaning of our whole society can remove this sickness from our soul.

For there is another kind of violence, slower but just as deadly, destructive as the shot or the bomb in the night. This is the violence of institutions; indifference and inaction and slow decay. This is the violence that afflicts the poor, that poisons relations between men because their skin has different colors. This is a slow destruction of a child by hunger, and schools without books and homes without heat in the winter.

This is the breaking of a man's spirit by denying him the chance to stand as a father and as a man among other men. And this too afflicts us all. I have not come here to propose a set of specific remedies, nor is there a single set. For a broad and adequate outline we know what must be done. When you teach a man to hate and fear his brother, when you teach that he is a lesser man because of his color or his beliefs or the policies he pursues, when you teach that those who differ from you threaten your freedom or your job or your family, then you also learn to confront others not as fellow citizens but as enemies—to be met not with cooperation but with conquest, to be subjugated and mastered.

We learn, at the last, to look at our brothers as aliens, men with whom we share a city, but not a community, men bound to us in common dwelling, but not in common effort. We learn to share only a common fear—only a common desire to retreat from each other—only a common impulse to meet disagreement with force. For all this there are no final answers.

Yet we know what we must do. It is to achieve true justice among our fellow citizens. The question is now what programs we should seek to enact. The question is whether we can find in our own midst and in our own hearts that leadership of human purpose that will recognize the terrible truths of our existence.

We must admit the vanity of our false distinctions among men and learn to find our own advancement in the search for the advancement of all. We must admit in ourselves that our own children's future cannot be built on the misfortunes of others. We must recognize that this short life can neither be ennobled or enriched by hatred or revenge.

Our lives on this planet are too short and the work to be done too great to let this spirit flourish any longer in our land. Of course we cannot vanish it with a program, nor with a resolution.

But we can perhaps remember—even if only for a time—that those who live with us are our brothers, that they share with us the same short movement of life, that they seek—as we do—nothing but the chance to live out their lives in purpose and happiness, winning what satisfaction and fulfillment they can.

Surely this bond of common faith, this bond of common goal, can begin to teach us something. Surely we can learn, at least, to look at those around us as fellow men and surely we can begin to work a little harder to bind up the wounds among us and to become in our hearts brothers and countrymen once again.

Robert F. Kennedy California Primary Victory Speech
Ambassador Hotel, Los Angeles
June 5, 1968

Thank you very much. . . . I want to first express my high regard to Don Drysdale, who pitched his sixth straight shut-out tonight, and I hope that we have as good fortune in our campaign.

Could I express my appreciation to a number of people first? To Jesse Unruh for all he did, and I express my appreciation to him for his friendship and his help during this campaign and for his continued perseverance and his effort and for all of those who have been associated with him. I'll always be very grateful.

And if I could also express my appreciation to a number of other people, if you'd just bear with me for a moment—I'd like to express my appreciation to Steve Smith, who was ruthless but has been effective, and I just want to say how much—how grateful I am to him, to his wife, my sister Jean, to my sister Pat, and to my mother and all of those other Kennedys.

I want to express my gratitude to my dog Freckles, who's been maligned—and I don't care what they, as Franklin Roosevelt said, I don't care what they say about me, but when they start to attack my dog—I'm not doing this in the order of importance, but I also want to thank my wife, Ethel. And her patience during this whole effort was fantastic. Thank you very much.

Freckles is going home to bed. He thought very early that we were going to win, so he retired.

I also want to thank Tom—point out Tom Reese, who is here and an early supporter. I want to thank a number of other people, if I may. All of those of you who worked so hard in this campaign. All of the students who worked across this state. The members of my delegation, our delegation, who also worked so diligently and with such unselfishness across the state on my behalf and on behalf of this cause that we're involved in.

I want to thank Cesar Chavez, who was here a little earlier. And Bert Corona, who also worked with him, and all of those Mexican Americans who were such supporters of mine.

And Dolores Huerta, who is an old friend of mine and has worked with the union, to thank her and tell her how much I appreciate her coming tonight. We have certain obligations and responsibilities to our fellow citizens which we talked about during the course of this campaign, and I want to make it clear that if I'm elected President of the United States, with your help, I intend to keep it up.

I want to also thank all my friends in the black community who made such an effort in this campaign. With such a high percentage voting today, I think it really made a major difference for me. I want to express my appreciation to them.

To my old friend, if I may, to Rafer Johnson, who's here. And to Rosey Grier, who said that he'd take care of anybody who didn't vote for me. In a kind way, because that's what we are in our campaign. Smile.

And I want to also, if I may, to just take a moment more of your time to express my appreciation to Paul Schrade, from the UAW, who worked so hard, and all the other members of the labor organizations and members of the labor unions. I am very grateful to him for what he's done and the effort that he's made on behalf of the working man here in the state of California. I'm very, very appreciative.

I'm very grateful for the votes that I received and

that all of you worked on behalf of the agricultural areas of the state as well as in the city. I think it indicates quite clearly—as well as in the suburbs—I think it indicates quite clearly what we could do here in the United States.

The vote here in the state of California, the vote in the state of South Dakota—here is the most urban state of any of the states of our union, South Dakota, the most rural state of any of the states of our union—we were able to win them both. I think that we can end the divisions within the United States.

What I think is—what I think is quite clear is that we *can* work together in the last analysis, and that what has been going on within the United States over the period of the last three years—the divisions, the violence, the disenchantment with our society, the divisions whether it's between blacks and whites, between the poor and the more affluent, or between age groups or over the war in Vietnam—that we can start to work together, that we are a great country, and an unselfish country, and a compassionate country. And I intend to make that my basis for running in the period of the next few months.

Ladies and gentlemen, if I can just take a moment

more of your time because everybody must be dying from the heat. But what I think all of these primaries have indicated—if I can just take a minute or two minutes more of your time—what all of these primaries have indicated and all of the party caucuses have indicated, whether they occurred in Colorado or Idaho or Iowa, wherever they occurred, it was the people in the Democratic Party and the people in the United States want a change.

And that change can come about only if they—those who are delegates in Chicago—recognize the importance of what has happened here in the state of California, what has happened in South Dakota, what happened in New Hampshire, what happened across the rest of this country.

The country wants to move in a different direction. We want to deal with our own problems within our own country, and we want peace in Vietnam.

I congratulate Senator McCarthy and those who have been associated with him in their efforts that they have started in New Hampshire and carried through to the primary here in the state of California. The fact is that all of us are involved in this great effort, and it's a great effort not on behalf of the Democratic Party, it's a great effort on behalf of the United States, on behalf of our own people, on behalf of mankind all around the globe and the next generation.

And I would hope—I would hope now that the California primary is finished, now that these primaries are over, that we can now concentrate on having a dialogue or a debate, I hope, between the vice president and perhaps myself on what direction we want to go in the United States. What we're going to do in the rural areas of our country, what we're going to do for those who still suffer within the United States from hunger, what we're going to do around the rest of the globe, and whether we're going to continue the policies that have been so unsuccessful in Vietnam, of American troops and American marines carrying the major burden of that conflict. I do not want to, and I think we should move in a different direction.

So I thank all of you who made this possible this evening. All of the effort that you made and all of the people whose names I haven't mentioned but who did all the work at the precinct level, who got out the vote, who brought forth all of the effort that's required.

I was a campaign manager eight years ago. I know

what a difference that kind of an effort and that kind of commitment make. So I thank all of you.

Mayor Yorty has just sent me a message that we've been here too long already.

So my thanks to all of you, and now it's on to Chicago and let's win there.

Tribute to Robert F. Kennedy
Senator Edward M. Kennedy
St. Patrick's Cathedral
New York City
June 8, 1968

On behalf of Mrs. Robert Kennedy, her children and the parents and sisters of Robert Kennedy, I want to express what we feel to those who mourn with us today in this Cathedral and around the world. We loved him as a brother and father and son. From his parents, and from his older brothers and sisters—Joe, Kathleen and Jack—he received inspiration which he passed on to all of us. He gave us strength in time of trouble, wisdom in time of uncertainty, and sharing in time of happiness. He was always by our side.

Love is not an easy feeling to put into words. Nor is loyalty, or trust or joy. But he was all of these. He loved life completely and lived it intensely.

A few years back, Robert Kennedy wrote some words about his own father and they expressed the way we in his family feel about him. He said of what his father meant to him:

"What it really all adds up to is love—not love as it is described with such facility in popular magazines, but the kind of love that is affection and respect, order, encouragement, and support. Our awareness of this was an incalculable source of strength, and because real love is something unselfish and involves sacrifice and giving, we could not help but profit from it.

"Beneath it all, he has tried to engender a social conscience. There were wrongs which needed attention. There were people who were poor and who needed help. And we have a responsibility to them and to this country. Through no virtues and accomplishments of our own, we have been fortunate enough to be born in the United States under the most comfortable conditions. We, therefore, have a responsibility to others who are less well off."

This is what Robert Kennedy was given. What he leaves us is what he said, what he did and what he stood for. . . .

My brother need not be idealized, or enlarged in death beyond what he was in life, to be remembered simply as a good and decent man, who saw wrong and tried to right it, saw suffering and tried to heal it, saw war and tried to stop it.

Those of us who loved him and who take him to his rest today, pray that what he was to us and what he wished for others will someday come to pass for all the world.

As he said many times, in many parts of this nation, to those he touched and who sought to touch him: *"Some men see things as they are and say why. I dream things that never were and say why not."*

Acknowledgments

My first duty here is to thank Simon & Schuster executive editor Stuart Roberts, publisher Sean Manning, and CEO Jonathan Karp. They gave me this assignment to take my work as a Robert F. Kennedy biographer to meet the occasion of his centennial. And I want to thank my wife, Kathleen Matthews, as before, for everything.

About the Author

CHRIS MATTHEWS anchored *Hardball* for a generation. He was Washington bureau chief for the *San Francisco Examiner* and a nationally syndicated columnist. Before that he was a speechwriter for President Jimmy Carter and later a senior aide to Speaker of the House Thomas P. "Tip" O'Neill Jr.

He is a graduate of Holy Cross and attended graduate school at the University of North Carolina at Chapel Hill, where he studied economics. He was a US Peace Corps volunteer, serving for two years as a trade development advisor in Africa.

Matthews holds thirty-four degrees from American institutions of higher learning. He teaches each year at Fulbright University Vietnam.

ALSO BY CHRIS MATTHEWS

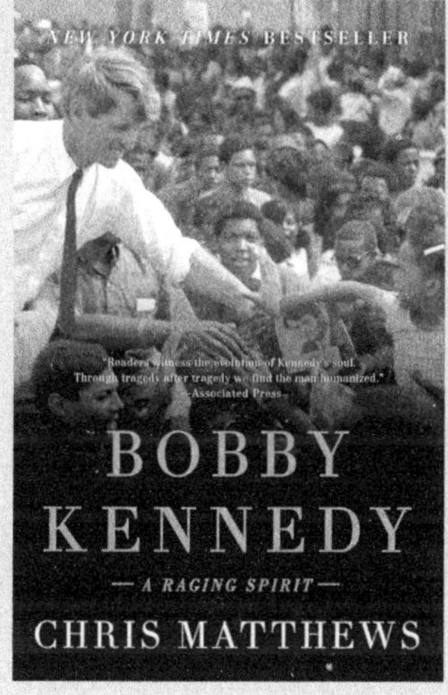